# The Way to Heaven

# The Way to Heaven

by
**John MacArthur, Jr.**

**WORD OF GRACE COMMUNICATIONS**
P.O. Box 4000
Panorama City, CA 91412

**Library of Congress Cataloging in Publication Data**

MacArthur, John, 1939-
    The way to heaven / by John MacArthur, Jr.
       p.    cm.    —(John MacArthur's Bible studies)
    Rev. ed. of: Which way to heaven? c1985.
    Includes indexes.
    ISBN 0-8024-5357-0
    1. Sermon on the mount.   2. Bible.  N.T.   Matthew VII, 13-29--
Criticism, interpretation, etc.   3. Salvation—Biblical teaching.
I. MacArthur, John, 1939-   Which way to heaven?   II. Title.
III. Series: MacArthur, John, 1939-    Bible studies.
    BT380.2.M324   1988
226'.906—dc19                                87-31182
                                                      CIP

1 2 3 4 5 6 7 Printing/LC/Year 93 92 91 90 89 88

*Printed in the United States of America*

# Contents

These Bible studies are taken from messages delivered by Pastor-Teacher John MacArthur, Jr., at Grace Community Church in Panorama City, California. These messages have been combined into a 5-tape album entitled *The Way to Heaven*. You may purchase this series either in an attractive vinyl cassette album or as individual cassettes. To purchase these tapes, request the album *The Way to Heaven*, or ask for the tapes by their individual GC numbers. Please consult the current price list; then, send your order, making your check payable to:

WORD OF GRACE COMMUNICATIONS
P.O. Box 4000
Panorama City, CA 91412

Or call the following toll-free number:
1-800-55-GRACE

# 1
## Which Way to Heaven?

### Outline

Introduction
A. The Choice
  1. Moses
  2. Joshua
  3. Jeremiah
  4. Elijah
  5. Jesus
B. The Contrast
  1. Defined
  2. Demonstrated
  3. Declared

Lesson
I. The Two Gates
  A. The Narrow Gate
    1. You must enter
      a) The command from Jesus
      b) The challenge to the Jews
    2. You must enter the narrow gate
      a) The basis of salvation denounced
      b) The basis of salvation defined
      c) The basis of salvation determined
    3. You must enter the narrow gate alone
      a) The difficulty recognized
        (1) Searching wholeheartedly
        (2) Striving wholeheartedly
      b) The diligence required
    4. You must enter the narrow gate unencumbered
      a) Illustrated
      b) Implemented

## Introduction

In Matthew 7 the Sermon on the Mount comes to a climax. That climax is stated in verses 13-14; the remainder of the sermon in chapter 7 is simply an expansion of those two verses. "Enter in at the narrow gate; for wide is the gate, and broad is the way, that leadeth to destruction, and many there be who go in that way; because narrow is the gate, and hard is the way, which leadeth unto life, and few there be that find it."

### A. The Choice

That is a provocative statement by the Lord. It is the point that He had emphasized in the first part of His masterful sermon, beginning in chapter 5. He brought the whole sermon to the climax of a decision. In verses 13-14 He talks about two gates, bringing an individual to two roads, leading to two destinations, populated by two different crowds. The Lord focused on the inevitable decision that must be made regarding what He had already spoken about in the Sermon on the Mount. Someone appropriately said that all of life concentrates on man at the crossroads. That is true. From the time we are old enough to make independent decisions, life becomes a matter of constant decision making. Every day we make decisions. We decide what time we will wake up, what we will eat, where we will go, and what we will do. We choose roads all the way through life, so it is fair to say that life consists of man at the crossroads. Ultimately and inevitably, there is a final choice you must make about where you will spend eternity. The Lord speaks of the choice in Matthew 7:13-14.

God has always made the effort to bring people to make that choice. There is always an option, so there is always a choice. The ultimate choice is what God is most concerned about.

1. Moses

   God confronts the children of Israel through Moses in Deuteronomy 30. He said, "I have set before you life and death, blessing and cursing; therefore, choose life, that both thou and thy seed may live" (v. 19). God gave the people of Israel an ultimate choice: life and good or death and evil. He called them to make a decision for one or the other.

2. Joshua

   Through Joshua, whom the people had followed into the Promised Land, the Israelites were given a choice: "Choose you this day whom ye will serve, whether the gods which your fathers served . . . but as for me and my house, we will serve the Lord" (Josh. 24:15).

3. Jeremiah

   God told Jeremiah, "Unto this people thou shalt say, Thus saith the Lord, Behold, I set before you the way of life, and the way of death" (Jer. 21:8).

4. Elijah

   When Elijah is on Mount Carmel in 1 Kings 18:21, he calls for the Israelites to make a decision: "How long halt ye between two opinions? If the Lord be God, follow him; but if Baal, then follow him." The ultimate choice is in view.

### 5. Jesus

In John 6 we read that many people followed Jesus and called themselves His disciples (as implied by vv. 60-61). But in verse 66, many of them turn their backs and no longer follow Him. Verses 67-68 say, "Then said Jesus unto the twelve, Will ye also go away? Then Simon Peter answered him, Lord, to whom shall we go? Thou hast the words of eternal life." Peter articulated his choice.

Some people walked away from Jesus, and others stayed with Him. Simeon said of Jesus, "Behold, this child is set for the fall and rising again of many in Israel" (Luke 2:34). Jesus is the crux of every person's destiny. The choice is made at the crossroads of Christ: choose life or death. Essentially that is what Jesus is saying in Matthew 7:13-14. The choice is clear-cut. There are only two choices: the narrow way or the wide way. There are no other alternatives.

## B. The Contrast

### 1. Defined

Let me add a footnote. The contrast is not between religion and paganism. Many people interpret Matthew 7:13-14 that way. They say the narrow way is the way of Christianity, which goes to heaven, and the broad way goes to hell. Jesus, however, was not contrasting Christians to immoral people on their way to hell. He was contrasting two kinds of religion. Both roads are marked "the way to heaven." Satan doesn't mark the broad way "the way to hell"; that wouldn't be deceptive. We are not looking at a contrast between righteousness and obvious unrighteousness but between divine righteousness and human righteousness.

Matthew 7:13-14 compares true, divine religion to false, human religion. For example, the problem of the Pharisees was that they "trusted in themselves that they were righteous" (Luke 18:9). Their religion was inadequate. Every person makes a choice. Either you believe you're good enough on your own—or through your system of religion—to make it to heaven, or you know you're not good enough, and you cast yourself on the mercy of God through Christ. Those are the only two systems of religion in the world. Jesus was saying, "There are two roads marked to heaven. One is the narrow road of divine righteousness; the other is the broad road of human righteousness."

The Jewish leaders, however, taught that a person could make it to heaven by his own efforts. That's why they were shocked when the apostle Paul said, "By the deeds of the law there shall no flesh be justified in [God's] sight" (Rom. 3:20). Paul says in verse 19 that the law came "that every mouth may be stopped, and all the world may become guilty before God." The law showed man his sinfulness. But when self-righteous, ego-centered man saw that he was sinful by the standards of the law, he didn't want to face his wickedness. Instead, he set the law aside, reinvented a new system that accommodated his shortcomings, and affirmed in his own mind that he was righteous. His righteousness became dependent on human achievement. The Lord's purpose in preaching the Sermon on the Mount was to break that kind of system. He showed that human achievement does not work.

2. Demonstrated

The Pharisees never got the message. Take note of the prayer of the Pharisee in Luke 18: "God, I thank thee that I am not as other men are. . . . I fast twice in the week; I give tithes of all that I possess" (vv. 11-12). Not once did the Pharisee express a need to God. He didn't believe he had any needs; he believed he was righteous. Near him a man pounded on his breast and said, "God, be merciful to me a sinner" (v. 13). Jesus said that man went home justified, not the Pharisee (v. 14).

3. Declared

Jesus wants to bring a person to the point where he realizes that in his flesh he is utterly incapable of pleasing God. He wants a person to be in desperation, with a broken spirit, meek and mournful, crying out for righteousness from God. The Jewish leaders believed they were on their way to heaven, but Jesus forced them to reconsider and make a decision. Every one of us has to make that decision. In Matthew 7:13-14 the choice is crystallized. There are two gates: the wide and the narrow. There are two ways: the broad and the narrow. There are two destinations: life and destruction. There are two groups of travelers: the few and the many.

The rest of Matthew 7 contains more contrasts. In verses 16-20 there are two kinds of trees: the good and the bad. Verses 24-27 say there are two builders: the wise and the foolish. There are two foundations: the rock and the sand. There are also two houses and two elements to the storm. At the climax of the Sermon on the Mount, a clear-cut decision is the issue. Jesus does not want compliments for His ethics. He does not want people to postpone applying the requirements; He wants a response from people. He forces us to make a decision.

There are four contrasts I want you to see in Matthew 7:13-14.

**Lesson**

I. THE TWO GATES

In verse 13 Jesus says, "Enter in at the narrow gate; for wide is the gate . . . that leadeth to destruction." In verse 14 He says, "Narrow is the gate . . . which leadeth unto life." He mentioned the narrow gate twice and the wide gate once. There are only two gates. Both roads say they point to salvation and God; both say they point to the kingdom, glory, and blessing. Both roads say they point to heaven, but only one goes there. One road is the route to self-righteousness; the other is the way of divine righteousness. Before you get on one of the roads, you have to go through a gate.

A. The Narrow Gate

Because the crux of interpreting Matthew 7:13-14 is in understanding the narrow gate, I want to focus on it and develop the concept that is involved in it.

12

1. You must enter

   a) The command from Jesus

   Jesus says in verse 13, "Enter in at the narrow gate."
   There is a sense of urgency in this aorist imperative.
   It demands action right away. "Enter now," He said.
   "This is the time to enter; that is what God is calling
   for. You must do it. It is not an option; it is a com-
   mand."

   b) The challenge to the Jews

   The Lord Jesus had been teaching His Jewish listeners about a narrow way of life. Their way of life toler-
   ated sin. They had all kinds of laws and standards
   beyond those of God. They had invented a man-
   made system. Jesus in effect told them, "You've got
   to get rid of that system. This is the way." He nar-
   rowed down the way a person should live so that by
   the time He came to Matthew 7:12, He had presented
   a confined approach to living to the glory of God. His
   audience understood that He was talking about a
   narrow, prescribed way. According to the end of
   chapter 7, Jesus "taught them as one having authority" (v. 29). Jesus didn't merely quote all the teach-
   ings of the Jewish rabbis; He explained the specifics
   of God's law. Compared to the Judaistic system, Jesus' way was narrow. He said that they must enter
   by the narrow way if they wanted to be in His kingdom. He demanded immediate action. He gave an
   absolute command without an alternative. It is not
   enough to listen to the preaching about the gate or to
   admire the ethics Jesus taught; one must enter the
   gate.

   Jesus said you cannot enter the kingdom unless you
   come on the terms He described. You must abandon
   your self-righteousness. You must see yourself as a beg-
   gar in spirit (Matt. 5:3), mourning over sin (v. 4), meek
   before a holy God (v. 5), and hungering and thirsting
   for righteousness (v. 6). You must enter on His terms.
   Hell will be full of people who admired the Sermon on
   the Mount. You must *enter* the gate.

2. You must enter the narrow gate

Jesus said there is a wide gate, but He didn't tell us to enter it, because it leads to destruction (Matt. 7:13). If you are going to be in the kingdom, you have to go through the narrow gate. You can't just admire it.

a) The basis of salvation denounced

The gate to the kingdom is narrow. People sometimes say, "Christianity doesn't leave room for anyone else's view of salvation." That is correct. But it is not that way because Christians are selfish or egotistical; God has given only one way for people to be saved. If God said there were forty-eight ways to be saved, I would preach all forty-eight. But there is only one way to be saved.

b) The basis of salvation defined

Acts 4:12 says, "Neither is there salvation in any other; for there is no other name under heaven given among men, whereby we must be saved." Jesus said "I am the bread of life" (John 6:35) and, "I am the way, the truth, and the life" (John 14:6). In John 10 Jesus says that He is "the door of the sheep" (v. 7) and that "he that entereth not by the door . . . but climbeth up some other way, the same is a thief and a robber" (v. 1). First Timothy 2:5 says, "There is one God, and one mediator between God and men, the man, Christ Jesus."

c) The basis of salvation determined

Christ is the only way to salvation. The way is narrow. There are no alternatives. You must enter by an act of the will and an act of faith; you have to enter on God's terms through God's prescribed gate. Christ is that gate (John 10:9). He is the only way. God has the right to determine the basis of salvation, and He has determined that it is through Jesus Christ alone.

3. You must enter the narrow gate alone

The fact that you must enter the narrow gate alone is implied in the text. The word *narrow* in verses 13-14 gives the idea that the gate is very narrow. In fact, some Bible commentators say that the best comparable contemporary idea would be that of a turnstile. A person has to go through a turnstile alone. The passageway through a turnstile is narrow; its metal arms don't allow more than one person through at a time. If a group of people are in a hurry to go in or out, they can't go through together. They have to go through one at a time. That's the way it is with the narrow gate. People don't come into the kingdom of Christ in groups.

The Jewish people believed that they were all on the road to heaven together because of their Abrahamic heritage and circumcision. There are some people who are sure they will go to heaven together. But groups can't go through the turnstile to heaven. People have to go through on an individual basis. Salvation is individual; people have never been saved in pairs. Sometimes one person's belief will influence another person to believe, but salvation is still exclusive and personal.

That can be hard for us, because our lives are usually spent doing things with a crowd. We do what other people do and belong to part of a group or system. Yet Christ in effect said, "To come into My kingdom, you're going to have to make a decision by yourself." To a Pharisee, that meant having to say good-bye to his friends and leaving the legalistic system of religion he adhered to. There is a price to pay. For the Jewish people, it isn't enough to claim Abrahamic heritage or depend on circumcision. It isn't enough for a person to say, "I was born into a Christian family and have gone to church all my life." People don't come into the kingdom in groups; they come in by an individual act of faith. You must enter the narrow gate, and you must enter it alone.

*a*) The difficulty recognized

It is difficult to enter the narrow gate. That shocks some of us; because we often hear that it is easy to become saved. Some say all you have to do is just believe, sign a card, walk the aisle, raise your hand, or go to the prayer room. The problem is that when people believe they're saved through doing those things they aren't on the right road—they didn't go through the narrow gate. It's difficult to become saved. Let me show you why.

(1) Searching wholeheartedly

The last part of Matthew 7:14 says about the narrow gate and the narrow way, "Few there be that find it." That implies people aren't even going to know about the narrow way unless they are looking for it. God said through an Old Testament prophet, "Ye shall seek me, and find me, when ye shall search for me with all your heart" (Jer. 29:13). No one ever slipped and fell into the kingdom of God. I don't believe it's easy to be saved. That's cheap grace or easy believism. Matthew 7:14 says, "Few there be that find it." You have to search for the narrow way.

(2) Striving wholeheartedly

Look at Luke 13, and I'll show you something that will shock you. In verse 22 we read that Jesus "went through the cities and villages, teaching, and journeying toward Jerusalem." From verse 23, we learn that the people who were with Jesus realized that not everyone was responding to His teaching. One of the people with Him said, "Lord, are there few that be saved?" The person who asked that question observed that not many people were responding to Christ. The answer our Lord gave implied why few become saved. He said, "Strive to enter in at the narrow gate" (v. 24). The word *strive* is the Greek word *agonizomai*, which means "to agonize." It is used in 1 Corinthians 9:25 to speak of an athlete agonizing to win a victory. That concept is spoken of in Colossians 4:12 with the words *laboring fervently* and in 1 Timothy 6:12 with the word *fight*. In other words, the Lord said that going through the narrow gate is agonizing. It demands fervent striving. He continues in Luke 13:24, "For many, I say unto you, will seek to enter in, and shall not be able."

It is difficult to be saved for two reasons. First, you've got to seek the narrow way. Second, even though you may be seeking, once you find out what it costs you must be willing to enter.

*b*) The diligence required

You don't become a Christian just because you walk an aisle; you don't become saved in a cheap and easy manner. Matthew 11:12 says, "The kingdom of heaven suffereth violence, and the violent take it by force." It is those who earnestly strive to enter the kingdom that get in. In Luke 16:16 the Lord says, "The kingdom of God is preached, and every man presseth into it." That is not what we hear today, but that's what Jesus taught. The kingdom is for those who seek it with all their hearts. It is for those who agonize to enter it. Their hearts need to be shattered over their sinfulness. The kingdom is for those who mourn in meekness, hunger and thirst for righteousness, and long for God to change their lives. It's not for people who come along in a cheap way, who want Jesus without altering their life-styles. We can't sleep our way into the kingdom; we have to make an earnest endeavor and display untiring energy. In fact, in John 16:33 Jesus says that "in the world ye shall have tribulation." It's not easy to become a Christian. Satan and his demons will fight you. In the power of God we must overcome Satan and the flesh to enter the kingdom.

One of Satan's pervasive lies in the world today is that it's easy to become a Christian. But it's not. You have to go through the narrow gate by yourself, agonizing over your sinfulness. You have to be broken in spirit. Some-

17

one might say, "That sounds like the religion of human achievement you talked about earlier." No; it's when you come with a broken spirit and recognize that you cannot enter heaven on your own that Christ pours into you grace upon grace to strengthen you to enter the narrow gate. In your brokenness, His power becomes your resource.

4. You must enter the narrow gate unencumbered

   *a)* Illustrated

   Have you ever noticed that you can't go through a turnstile with a lot of luggage? It's impossible. The narrow gate is the gate of self-denial. It does not admit superstars who want to carry in all their garbage. You need to strip off self-righteousness and sin, or you can't go through. The rich young ruler in Matthew 19 came to the gate. He said to Jesus, "Good Master, what good thing shall I do, that I may have eternal life?" (v. 16). The Lord went right to the heart of the problem and said, "If thou wilt be perfect, go and sell what thou hast, and give to the poor" (v. 21). Jesus hit the rich young ruler right where his extra baggage was. The man was trying to get through the narrow gate with his riches. He also had the baggage of self-righteousness, because he told the Lord that he had kept all the commandments (vv. 17-20). The rich young ruler couldn't get through the narrow gate with his riches and self-righteousness. Verse 22 says that "he went away sorrowful." He wasn't willing to deny himself and agonize over his sin. He didn't strip himself of his baggage.

   *b)* Implemented

   If you didn't go through the narrow gate the way you are supposed to, then you're on the wrong road. It doesn't matter whether the road *says* it goes to heaven or Jesus. You must have jettisoned self in order to enter. The Lord says in Matthew 18:3, "Except ye be converted, and become as little children, ye shall not enter into the kingdom of heaven." What characteristic does a little child have? Utter dependency. Someone once wrote, "Nothing in my hand I bring; simply to Thy cross I cling." Saving faith is not only an act of the mind; it involves stripping self in utter nakedness. It says, "God, be merciful to me, a sinner" (Luke 18:13). I believe that the Lord is dealing with the danger of easy believism in Matthew 7:13-14. Some people say, "Come to Jesus. It's so easy. Just believe and pray." There's nothing wrong with believing or praying, but those things do not bring true salvation when they occur in a vacuum. Becoming saved involves a difficult and radical admission that you are sinful and cannot commend yourself to God.

5. You must enter the narrow gate repentantly

You can't go through the narrow gate unless your heart is repentant over sin. You must turn from sin to serve the living God. When John the Baptist was exhorting people to receive the Messiah, many people came to be baptized because they wanted to have their sins cleansed. The Jewish people knew that preparing for the Messiah meant purging their hearts of sinfulness. Charles Hadden Spurgeon, the famous nineteenth-century English preacher, said, "You and your sins must separate or you and your God will never come together. No one sin may you keep; they must all be given up. They must be brought out like the Canaanish kings from the cave and be hanged up in the sun." You must turn from sin to God; there must be repentance in your heart.

6. You must enter the narrow gate in utter surrender

You have to come through the narrow gate in total abandonment to Christ. I do not believe that a person can be regenerated by adding Jesus Christ to his carnal activities. Salvation is not an addition to your life; it is a transformation of your life. The whole message of 1 John is that if you are truly redeemed, your life will manifest a transformation: you will confess sin, obedience will become a characteristic of your life, and you will manifest love. Salvation is marked by a changed life. Jesus said, "If ye continue in my word, then you are my disciples indeed" (John 8:31). If you believe you are a Christian but there is no sign of obedience in your life, then you are on the wrong road. Even if the road says it points to heaven and Jesus, without obedience you are not on the right path.

B. The Wide Gate

I don't need to say as much about the wide gate; it's obvious by contrast. Everyone can go through the wide gate together. You don't have to go through alone. There is nothing individualistic about it. There is no self-denial expected. You can bring all the baggage that you want: your immorality, lack of repentance, and lack of commitment to Christ. The wide gate is the gate of self-indulgence. Many people who claim to be Christians are totally self-indulgent. Pride, self-righteousness, self-indulgence, and all kinds of sins are welcome on the broad road. But if you have those things in your life, then you are not on the narrow road, because you can't get through the narrow gate with baggage.

## II. THE TWO WAYS

What are the two ways? Matthew 7:13 mentions the broad way, and Matthew 7:14 mentions the hard or confined way. Psalm 1 also talks about them: there is the way of the godly (vv. 1-3) and the way of the ungodly (vv. 4-5). Verse 6 tells the result of walking the ungodly way. The choices are the same as they have always been: you can either go the way of the godly or the way of the ungodly.

A. The Broad Way

Once you've come through the wide gate it's easy living. There is no precipice. There is plenty of room to stroll. There are no rules; no morality is particularly binding. There is room for diverse theology. There is tolerance of every conceivable sin, just as long as you "love" Jesus or are "religious." There are no boundaries. All the desires of the fallen heart are fed on that road. There is no need for a Beatitude attitude or a study of the Word of God. There is no need for internal moral standards. You can live with a mechanical kind of religiosity that is no more than hypocrisy. The wide way doesn't require you to have character; you can be like a dead fish floating downstream, letting the current do the work. Ephesians 2:2 calls the road "the course of this world." Proverbs 14:12 sums up the tragedy of the broad way: "There is a way which seemeth right unto a man, but the end thereof are the ways of death." The wide way has no standards except those made by men to fit into their comfortable system. But Psalm 1:6 warns, "The way of the ungodly shall perish."

B. The Narrow Way

1. Defined

Verse 14 talks about the hard or narrow way. The best translation is "a constricted way." It literally speaks of being confined to a narrow path on a precipice. That's why in Ephesians 5:15 Paul says, "See, then, that ye walk circumspectly." You must walk with your eyes open; the path is narrow, and it is hemmed in on both sides by the chastening hand of God. If you step off either side of the path, you will get rapped on your spiritual knuckles! The requirements are great, strict, and clear-cut; there is no room for deviation. You must desire in your heart to fulfill those requirements, knowing that if you fail, God will chasten you, lovingly forgive you, and set you on your feet again.

You may say, "If it's a hard, strict, and narrow way, then it might be something that I wouldn't want." The wonderful thing about walking the narrow path, however, is that all the difficulty of walking it is borne by Christ Himself. Jesus said, "My yoke is easy, and my burden is light" (Matt. 11:30). But be aware of what you are asking for if you decide to walk on the narrow way.

2. Depicted

a) Counting the cost

Luke 14:25-26 says, "There went great multitudes with him; and he turned, and said unto them, If any man come to me, and hate not his father, and mother, and wife, and children, and brethren, and sisters, yea, and his own life also, he cannot be my disciple." Jesus was saying, "If you want to be a Christian, you're going to have to step out of the crowd and say good-bye to everyone you love, or you can't be My disciple. Then you're going to have to pick up a cross and live a crucified life." If that was preached at a revival, how many people would come forward to accept Christ? The people who *should* come; the people who want to make the right kind of commitment.

Jesus continued His line of thought with some illustrations. He says in verse 28, "For which of you, intending to build a tower, sitteth not down first, and counteth the cost?" In other words, you shouldn't start building something without analyzing what it's going to cost. Jesus added, "What king, going to make war against another king, sitteth not down first, and consulteth whether he is able with ten thousand to meet him that cometh against him with twenty thousand?" (v. 31). Verse 33 says, "So, likewise, whosoever he is of you that forsaketh not all that he hath, cannot be my disciple."

*b*) Clarifying the challenge

Jesus drew a hard line. If you're not willing to say no to everything and walk that narrow path, you can't become a disciple of Christ. If you do walk the narrow walk, remember that it is God who enables you to do so. You can't walk the narrow path by yourself, but God will give you grace upon grace, and His strength will pour through your weakness so that you can make it. If you're willing to live the way God wants you to, then you're coming to Him the right way. Remember that you will be persecuted and face tribulation. Jesus told His disciples that "the time cometh, that whosoever killeth you will think that he doeth God service" (John 16:2). You're going to spend your life running from those who want to persecute you.

The narrow way can't be walked upon with bare feet. It's not a luscious meadow. The road is hard. Jesus never presented Christianity as a soft option for the weakhearted. You declare war on hell when you go through the narrow gate—and hell fights back. You must live your life with a Beatitude attitude; you must constantly deal with your pride and selfish desires. Jesus in essence said to Peter, "Follow Me. By the way, it will cost you your life" (John 21:15-19).

Are you coming to Christ on those terms? That's what the narrow way is like. It's hard, pressed, and confined. If you wander off the path, God will chasten you. You may say, "But it sounds so hard!" No, it's not hard because Jesus shoulders the burden for you.

## III. THE TWO DESTINATIONS

According to Matthew 7 the broad way "leadeth to destruction" (v. 13), and the narrow way "leadeth unto life" (v. 14). Moses, Joshua, Jeremiah, and Elijah all spoke of the way of life and the way of death (see p. 9). Psalm 1:6 says that the godly are blessed and "the ungodly shall perish." The word *destruction* in Matthew 7:13 refers to ultimate, eternal judgment in hell.

The Lord said that everyone ends up in one of two places. All the religions of the world (except the religion of divine accomplishment in Christ) will end up in the same place: "destruction." It's easy to go on the path that leads that way; you can take all you want with you. There are no standards. But when you reach the end of that path, things become rough. There are no restrictions and plenty of people along the way, but it ends in hell.

John Bunyan said that "the entrance of hell is from the portals of heaven." Some people are going to get a shock when they realize they are going to hell. On the other hand, the narrow way is going to open up into eternal bliss. The broad way narrows down into a terrible pit; the narrow way opens up into the fullness of an everlasting fellowship of joy with God. Eternal life isn't quantitative; it's qualitative. The choice is yours. Consider the destination of the way you choose—you will spend eternity there.

## IV. THE TWO CROWDS

Matthew 7:13 says, "Broad is the way, that leadeth to destruction, and many there be who go in that way." Verse 14 says,

23

"Hard is the way, which leadeth unto life, and few there be that find it." Most people are on the road of human achievement—the wrong road.

People often ask me, "Will heaven or hell have more people?" Jesus answered that question in Matthew 7:13-14. In the Old Testament there was always a remnant of believing people. The one time in God's redemptive history that will be unique is the Tribulation. According to Revelation 7, there will be an innumerable multitude of Gentiles redeemed out of every nation, language, and people (v. 9). There will also be redeemed people from the nation of Israel (vv. 4-8; Rom. 11:26). There will be a massive response to the gospel during the Tribulation. Many people will respond to Christ. But for this age, the response to Christ is small because people would rather hold onto their sin. Jesus said that people love darkness (John 3:19).

A. The Little Crowd on the Narrow Way

In Luke 12:32 Jesus says to His disciples, "Fear not, little flock." The word *little* represents the Greek word *micron.* From it we get the word *micro,* which means "something small." The same word is used in Matthew 13:32 of the mustard seed, which is the smallest of seeds. There have always been only a few people who seek the way to heaven with all their hearts. There are few people who agonize over their inability to enter heaven and are willing to count the cost of walking the narrow way. In fact, Jesus says in Matthew 22:14, "For many are called, but few are chosen."

B. The Large Crowd on the Broad Way

It's easy to choose the broad way; you just go with the crowd. You can try to add Jesus to your life, feel religious, and go to church. You can join a system of religion that says it points to heaven and that you need never deny yourself. Either way you will end up in disaster. In Luke 13 Jesus says, "Strive ["agonize"] to enter in at the narrow gate; for many, I say unto you, will seek to enter in, and shall not be able. When once the master of the house is risen up, and hath shut the door, and ye begin to stand outside, and to knock at the door, saying, Lord, Lord, open unto us; and he shall answer and say unto you, I know you not from where ye are; then shall ye begin to say, We have

24

eaten and have drunk in thy presence, and thou hast taught in our streets. But he shall say, I tell you, I know you not from where ye are; depart from me, all ye workers of iniquity. There shall be weeping and gnashing of teeth, when ye shall see Abraham, and Isaac, and Jacob, and all the prophets, in the kingdom of God. . . . And, behold, there are last who shall be first, and there are first who shall be last" (vv. 24-28, 30). Jesus was not talking about irreligious people; He referred to religious people who believed they were on the right road. I can't think of a more horrible scene than that of people who believe they are saved being locked out of heaven.

Jesus said many will go on the broad road (Matt. 7:13). In verses 22-23 Jesus says, "Many will say to me in that day, Lord, Lord, have we not prophesied in thy name? And in thy name have cast out demons? And in thy name done many wonderful works? And then will I profess unto them, I never knew you; depart from me, ye that work iniquity." People on the broad road are going to find out that they were not on the road to heaven. The door will be shut forever.

The way to heaven is narrow, but it's wide enough to take in the chief of sinners (1 Tim. 1:13, 15). You've got to enter the narrow gate alone. You can't escape the choice; you must make it. To make no choice means that you've made a choice —and you will face that decision.

### Focusing on the Facts

1. What significance does Matthew 7:13-14 have in the Sermon on the Mount? What do the verses following Matthew 7:13-14 do (see p. 8)?
2. What does the Lord focus on in Matthew 7:13-14 (see p. 8)?
3. Cite some examples from Scripture of God's offering people an ultimate choice. Ultimately, what two alternatives does every person have (see pp. 9-10)?
4. The contrast in Matthew 7:13-14 is not between religion and paganism. What is being contrasted (see p. 10)?
5. What did man do when he saw that he was sinful according to the law (see p. 11)?

6. What point does Jesus want to bring man to (see p. 11)?
7. What is similar about the narrow and wide roads? What is different about them (see p. 12)?
8. What is significant about the way Jesus said, "Enter in at the narrow gate" (Matt. 7:13; see p. 13)?
9. Using Scripture, support the fact that there is only one way to become saved. Who determined the basis of salvation (see p. 14)?
10. What is a good contemporary illustration that a person must enter the narrow gate alone (see p. 15)?
11. Explain why it is difficult to become saved. Support your answer with Scripture (see pp. 16-17).
12. What is one of Satan's pervasive lies today (see p. 17)?
13. To become saved, a person must go through the narrow gate without any baggage. What must a person strip himself of (see p. 18)?
14. You can't go through the narrow gate unless your heart is _____ over sin (see p. 19).
15. Salvation is not an _____ to your life; it is a _____ of your life (see p. 19).
16. What does a truly redeemed life manifest? Be specific (see p. 19).
17. Describe the "requirements" of going through the wide gate (see p. 20).
18. Describe the narrow way. What is it hemmed in by? What does God do if you fail the requirements of the narrow way (see p. 21)?
19. What is wonderful about walking the narrow way (see p. 21)?
20. Is there a cost to walking the narrow way? Explain (see pp. 21-22).
21. What do you declare war on when you go through the narrow gate? How must you live your life (see pp. 22-23)?
22. What does the narrow way open into? What does the broad way narrow down into (see p. 23)?
23. What will the response to Christ be like during the Tribulation (Rev. 7:4-9)? Why do only a few people choose to respond to Christ during this age (see p. 24)?
24. What will happen to people who add Jesus to their lives without denying themselves (Luke 13:24-28, 30; Matt. 7:22-23; see pp. 24-25)?

# Pondering the Principles

1. Have you ever examined yourself to make sure that you are coming to heaven on God's terms? In Matthew 5, at the beginning of the Sermon on the Mount, Jesus specifies those terms: you must be poor in spirit (admit that you are spiritually bankrupt and helpless to enter heaven on your own; v. 3), sad over your sin (v. 4), meek (patient and submissive; v. 5), and hungering and thirsting for righteousness (v. 6). Are all four characteristic of your life? Can you honestly say that your life changed at the time you acknowledged Christ as your Savior? If not, then you have not come through the narrow gate that leads to heaven. Confess your sinfulness to God now, and ask for the righteousness that Christ's blood has made available for you. Give God control of your life, and be obedient to Him. If you did come through the narrow gate, thank God for making available to you a way to receive eternal life.

2. Read Psalm 1:1-6. According to verse 1, what kind of man is blessed by God? What characterizes a godly person (v. 2)? What is the result if a person walks righteously (v. 3)? According to verse 4, the ungodly "are like the chaff which the wind driveth away." What does Matthew 3:12 say that Jesus will do with the chaff? What does Psalm 1:5-6 say about the ungodly? When you tell someone the gospel message, let him know the consequences of the choice that he makes about his eternal destiny.

# 2

# Beware of False Prophets—Part 1

**Outline**

Introduction
A. The Call Pronounced
    1. In the New Testament
    2. In the Old Testament
B. The Choices Presented
C. The Caution Proclaimed

Lesson
I. Warning
  A. The Definition
    1. The purpose of true prophets
    2. The problem of false prophets
      *a*) In the Old Testament
        (1) Jeremiah
        (2) Zechariah
      *b*) In the New Testament
  B. The Danger
    1. Declared
      *a*) By Peter
      *b*) By Jude
    2. Defined
      *a*) John
        (1) The shepherd
        (2) The hired laborer
        (3) The wolf
      *b*) Jude
        (1) The doubters
        (2) The endangered unbelievers
        (3) The cult members

C. The Deception
   1. The clothes of false prophets
      *a*) Imitate a true prophet's clothing
      *b*) Imitate a true shepherd's clothing
   2. The categories of false prophets
      *a*) The heretic
      *b*) The apostate
      *c*) The deceiver
   3. The characteristics of false prophets
      *a*) Their words
      *b*) Their ways
D. The Damnation
   1. The conversation detailed
   2. The condemnation detailed
      *a*) They will not be alone
      *b*) They will not be spared


**Introduction**


Matthew 7:15-20 is the text we will study in this lesson: "Beware of false prophets, who come to you in sheep's clothing, but inwardly they are ravening wolves. Ye shall know them by their fruits. Do men gather grapes of thorns, or figs of thistles? Even so, every good tree bringeth forth good fruit, but a corrupt tree bringeth forth bad fruit. A good tree cannot bring forth bad fruit, neither can a corrupt tree bring forth good fruit. Every tree that bringeth not forth good fruit is hewn down, and cast into the fire. Wherefore, by their fruits ye shall know them."

A. The Call Pronounced

   In the climax of the Sermon on the Mount the Lord presents us with an ultimate choice. Jesus says in Matthew 7:13-14, "Enter in at the narrow gate; for wide is the gate, and broad is the way, that leadeth to destruction, and many there be who go in that way; because narrow is the gate, and hard is the way, which leadeth unto life, and few there be that find it." The Lord is extending an invitation; He calls for a decision.

### 1. In the New Testament

That is not a unique passage, for the Lord calls for a decision elsewhere in Scripture. The compassionate, loving heart of Christ longs for people to enter into the right path. He wants people to forsake their sin and self-will and come repentantly to the only source of true righteousness. In Matthew 4:17 Jesus cries, "Repent; for the kingdom of heaven is at hand." In other words, "Turn around and go the other way." In Matthew 11:28 Jesus recognizes the burdens of sinfulness and impossible religious duties. He said, "Come unto me, all ye that labor and are heavy laden, and I will give you rest." In John 7 He says, "If any man thirst, let him come unto me, and drink" (v. 37). In addition Jesus said, "I am the bread of life" (John 6:35), "I am the good shepherd" (John 10:11), "I am the way, the truth, and the life" (John 14:6), and "I am the resurrection" (John 11:25). Jesus repeatedly offered an invitation for people to come to Him.

### 2. In the Old Testament

In the book of Isaiah we find a foreshadowing of the invitation of Christ: "Come now, and let us reason together, saith the Lord: though your sins be as scarlet, they shall be as white as snow; though they be red like crimson, they shall be as wool. If ye be willing and obedient . . ." (1:18-19). God has always wanted to wash away the sins of all people, but each person has to recognize his need for that before he will seek Him. A person's sins will never be white as snow until he realizes his sinfulness.

Another invitation appears in Isaiah 55: "Every one that thirsteth, come to the waters, and he that hath no money; come, buy and eat; yea, come, buy wine and milk without money and without price" (v. 1). In other words, when you recognize that you need to have your sins cleansed and that you have no resources to meet that need, then "come, buy wine and milk without money and without price." No one has anything to offer God; one comes to Him strictly on the merits of His good and gracious gift in Christ.

The invitation appears in both the Old and New Testaments. The end of the Bible even climaxes in a great, final invitation: "The Spirit and the bride say, Come. And let him that heareth say, Come. And let him that is athirst come. And whosoever will, let him take the water of life freely" (Rev. 22:17). The invitation appears throughout the Bible: "enter the narrow gate," "be converted," "come unto me," "if any man thirst, come without money and buy," "if your sins are as scarlet they will be white as snow," "the Spirit and the bride say, Come." The loving heart of God constantly beats in compassion toward people, desiring that they be saved (2 Pet. 3:9). In Matthew 23:37 Jesus weeps over the city of Jerusalem because the people will not come to Him.

The heart of God compassionately calls out to people. But I must add that the Lord's compassion has wrath in it. In fact, if you don't listen to God's call and come to Him the way He wants you to, then you are on the road to damnation. God's compassion is mingled with judgment. In His invitation the Lord is saying, "Love calls, and judgment tarries, but the time will come when love is set aside and judgment is imminent." We are to come to Him on the narrow way.

B.  The Choices Presented

Every man and woman stands at the crossroads. On one side is the narrow gate, the narrow way that leads to life. On the other side is the broad way that leads to damnation. Both ways say they point to heaven, but one is right and the other wrong. The narrow way is the religion of divine accomplishment, and the broad way is the religion of human achievement. You choose one or the other. It is not easy to get through the narrow gate. Matthew 7:14 says, "Few there be that find it." Once you've found it, you must agonize to enter into it.

C.  The Caution Proclaimed

One reason it is difficult to enter the narrow gate is that while you stand at the crossroads before the two gates, there are false prophets doing everything they can to push you the wrong way. Like spiritual traffic cops, they wave people onto the broad road that leads to damnation. That's why Jesus follows His invitation in Matthew 7:13-14 with a warning about false prophets: "Beware of false prophets" (v. 15). They stand at the crossroads, obscuring the narrow way and pushing people onto the broad way. And they do it successfully. If you don't believe that, verse 22 says that "many" will go along the broad way. Verse 13 says, "Many there be who go in that way."

Many people who complete the broad way will arrive at the end and say, "Lord, Lord, have we not prophesied in thy name? And in thy name have cast out demons? And in thy name done many wonderful works?" (v. 22). They will say, "We are religious!" But Jesus said, "Then will I profess unto them, I never knew you; depart from me, ye that work iniquity" (v. 23).

Many people will go on the wrong road because there are false prophets pushing them that way. In Matthew 7:15-20 Jesus is saying, "As you strive to enter that narrow gate, beware of those who try to mislead you."

**Lesson**

I. WARNING

In Matthew 7:15 Jesus says, "Beware of false prophets, who come to you in sheep's clothing, but inwardly they are ravening wolves."

**What Does the Bible Say About False Prophets?**

1. Warnings in the Old Testament

In the Pentateuch, penned by Moses under the inspiration of the Holy Spirit, we find God's instruction about false prophets in the earliest times of redemptive history. Deuteronomy 13:1-5 says, "If there arise among you a prophet, or a dreamer of dreams, and giveth thee a sign or a wonder, and the sign or the wonder come to pass, whereof he spoke unto thee, saying, Let us go after other gods, which thou hast not known, and let us serve them, thou shalt not hearken unto the words of that prophet, or that dreamer of dreams; for the Lord your God testeth you, to know whether ye love the Lord your God with all your heart and with all your soul. Ye shall walk after the Lord your God, and fear him, and keep his commandments, and obey his voice, and ye shall serve him, and cleave unto him. And that prophet, or that dreamer of dreams, shall be put to death, because he hath spoken to turn you away from the Lord your God, who brought you out of the land of Egypt, and redeemed you." In other words, "If you find a false prophet, kill him. He is deadly."

Isaiah 30:9-10 says, "This is a rebellious people, lying children, children who will not hear the law of the Lord: who say to the seers, See not; and to the prophets, Prophesy not unto us right things; speak unto us smooth things, prophesy deceits." Isaiah said that there will be some who want to prophesy deceits and others who want to hear false prophets. There is always a demand for false prophets because people do not want to hear the truth.

Jeremiah repeatedly warned about false prophets, starting in chapter 5 and continuing to chapter 23.

2. Warnings in the New Testament

Matthew 24:11 says, "Many false prophets shall rise, and shall deceive many." Notice the word *many*. Many false prophets will deceive many people. Multitudes will say, "Lord, Lord" (Matt. 7:22), but Jesus will say, "I don't know any of you" (v. 23). Many people will say, "But we have prophesied in your name!" (v. 22). False prophets will come to the same end that their followers do. They will claim that their deeds were done in the Lord's name, but their claim will not stand.

Matthew 24:24 says, "For there shall arise false Christs [Gk., *psuedochristos*], and false prophets, and shall show great signs and wonders, insomuch that, if it were possible, they shall deceive the very elect." There will be people who try to present themselves as Christ. They are phonies and liars.

Romans 16:17-18 says, "Now I beseech you, brethren, mark them who cause divisions and offenses contrary to the doctrine which ye have learned; and avoid them. For they that are such serve not our Lord Jesus Christ but their own body, and by good words and fair speeches deceive the hearts of the innocent." Paul told Timothy, "Some shall depart from the faith, giving heed to . . . doctrines of demons" (1 Tim. 4:1). Peter said, "There shall be false teachers among you, who secretly shall bring in destructive heresies" (2 Pet. 2:1). John said, "Test the spirits whether they are of God" (1 John 4:1).

The Bible warns us repeatedly about false prophets. There have been and will be many false prophets as long as we live on this earth. They will be here until the second coming of Christ.

There are four words I want to use to explain the warning Jesus gives in Matthew 7:15.

A. The Definition

What is a false prophet? Whom are we dealing with in Matthew 7:15? Let me give you some background information first.

1. The purpose of true prophets

Ever since the Fall of man (Gen. 3), every person has been hopelessly lost. Everyone has turned his back on God and has fled from Him. No one seeks God (Rom. 3:11). Every person runs to hell as fast as he can. As a result, God picked certain people, redeemed them, and used them to draw people's hearts back to God. Those people were His prophets. In both the Old and New Testaments, a prophet was known by two things: he had a divine commission and a divine message. He was called by God, and he gave God's message.

A true prophet was God's voice. In Exodus 4 Moses argues with God about his speech problems. The Lord in effect said, "Don't worry about what you're going to say; I will put my words in your mouth" (vv. 10-12). Prior to that God had called to Moses from a burning bush and commissioned him to become a prophet (Ex. 3:1-10). The Lord chose Moses and gave him the content of His message. That consummated Moses' role as a prophet. He was God's man; he spoke God's message. Yet as soon as God assigned His true prophets to be shepherds to draw wayward sheep back to Himself, Satan brought along counterfeits.

2. The problem of false prophets

a) In the Old Testament

When you study the Old Testament, you continuously see the trouble that false prophets caused. They were everywhere in the Old Testament era, just as they are today.

(1) Jeremiah

We could spend days studying what Jeremiah said about false prophets. He talked about them more than anyone else did in the Bible. In Jeremiah 14:14 he says, "Then the Lord said unto me, The prophets prophesy lies in my name, I sent them not, neither have I commanded them, neither spoke unto them." God said that false prophets were deceiving the people. And they were doing a good job of it. In Jeremiah 5:31 the Lord says, "The prophets prophesy falsely . . . and my people love to have it so." The people accepted what the false prophets said because the false prophets tickled the people's ears. That's the way it will be in the future: men will "heap to themselves teachers, having itching ears" (2 Tim. 4:3). False prophets give platitudes that people want to hear, which are nothing but lies.

Jeremiah 23:14-16 says, "I have seen also in the prophets of Jerusalem an horrible thing; they commit adultery, and walk in lies; they strengthen also the hands of evildoers, that none doth return from his wickedness; they are all of them unto me like Sodom, and its inhabitants like Gomorrah. Therefore, thus saith the Lord of hosts concerning the prophets, Behold, I will feed them with wormwood, and make them drink the water

of gall; for from the prophets of Jerusalem is pro-
faneness gone forth into all the land. Thus saith
the Lord of hosts, Hearken not unto the words of
the prophets that prophesy unto you. They make
you vain; they speak a vision of their own heart,
and not out of the mouth of the Lord." False
prophets make men proud; they appeal to their
egos. They are all evil, fleshly, adulterous, and
they strengthen the hands of evildoers. False
prophets are evil; they say what people want to
hear.

Finally, in Jeremiah 23:21, 28 God says, "I have
not sent these prophets, yet they ran; I have not
spoken to them, yet they prophesied. . . . The
prophet that hath a dream, let him tell a dream;
and he that hath my word, let him speak my
word faithfully." In other words, "I don't want to
silence all prophets, just the false ones."

(2) Zechariah

Zechariah 11:16 gives a vivid picture of a false
shepherd: "For, lo, I will raise up a shepherd in
the land, who shall not visit those that are cut
off." Can you imagine a shepherd that doesn't
bother to find lost sheep? The verse continues,
"Neither shall [he] seek the young one, nor heal
that which is broken, nor feed that which stand-
eth still, but he shall eat the flesh of the fat, and
tear their claws in pieces." The false shepherd described here won't help a stray lamb or injured
sheep. Rather, he eats the fat of the sheep. The
fact that he tears "their claws in pieces" means
that he will literally rip the hooves apart to get every little morsel of meat.

God said, "Woe to the idol shepherd that leaveth
the flock! The sword shall be upon his arm, and
upon his right eye; his arm shall be completely
dried up, and his right eye shall be utterly dark-
ened" (Zech. 11:17). The false shepherd described in Zechariah 11:16-17 is the Antichrist,
whom God will judge. The Antichrist is the pro-

totype of all false prophets. He cares nothing for the sheep. He masquerades as if he were Christ but tears apart the flock.

The scribes and Pharisees were classic examples of false shepherds. They crucified Jesus because He mercilessly unmasked them. They paraded themselves as if they were godly, but they were rapacious and self-serving. They took advantage of people for personal gain.

*b*) In the New Testament

False prophets were called many things in the New Testament: "false brethren" (2 Cor. 11:26), "false apostles" (2 Cor. 11:13), "false teachers" (2 Pet. 2:1), false speakers (1 Tim. 4:2), and "false Christs" (Matt. 24:24). The Greek word for "false" in those verses is *pseudo*, which means "sham" or "phony."

Despite the fact that false prophets are liars, they always have an audience. Jesus says in John 8:45, "Because I tell you the truth, ye believe me not." The people Jesus spoke to couldn't hear the truth because they listened for lies. Why? They were "of [their] father the devil . . . he is a liar, and the father of it" (John 8:44). In Jeremiah 5:31 God says, "The prophets prophesy falsely . . . and my people love to have it so." People "heap to" ("accumulate for," NASB*) themselves teachers who lie (2 Tim. 4:3). False prophets will always have an audience.

B. The Danger

1. Declared

Matthew 7:15 not only tells us to beware of false prophets; it tells us why we are to watch out for them: they are dangerous. We can all be easy prey for false prophets. The word *beware* in verse 15 lets us know they are dangerous. Whenever I see the word *beware* on a sign, I am careful. I don't want to run into a gorilla or a huge dog

---

*New American Standard Bible.

or be electrocuted. *Beware* is a strong word; the Greek word for it means "hold your mind away from." Don't ever expose your mind to the influence of false prophets. Don't pay attention to them; they pervert the mind and poison the soul.

*a*) By Peter

Second Peter 2:2 tells us the result of their work: "Many shall follow their pernicious ways." Many people will take the broad road, believing they are religious, but they are following a pied piper who will lead them to damnation. Peter called false prophets "natural brute beasts" (v. 12), "spots . . . and blemishes" (v. 13), and beguilers of unstable souls (v. 14). He said that "they allure through the lusts of the flesh" (v. 18).

*b*) By Jude

Jude calls false prophets "brute beasts" (v. 10). He said that they "are spots [or "scabs"] in your love feasts" (v. 12) and that they flatter people for personal gain (v. 16). They are dangerous and clever.

You would be better off embracing a cobra or crawling in bed with a hungry lion than being near a false prophet. It would be better for you to drink a bottle of poison; then you would only be affected physically. False prophets pervert the mind.

2. Defined

Why are false prophets so dangerous? Matthew 7:15 says "inwardly they are ravening wolves." They don't appear to be wolves, but that's what they are. The fact that false prophets are ravenous wolves appears in the Old Testament, too, in Ezekiel 22:27-28.

*a*) John

The wolf was the primary enemy of sheep in Palestine. Wolves roamed the hills. When one spotted a flock, it would sneak up on it. Then it would snatch a sheep and rip it to shreds. Sheep were totally defenseless against a wolf. In John 10, when Jesus talks about the characteristics of good shepherds, He says they are always on the alert for wolves. A shepherd who cares for his sheep always watches after them.

John 10 talks about three kinds of characters that deal with a flock.

(1) The shepherd

A good shepherd cares for his sheep. He will give his life for them (v. 11). He will do anything to keep them from a wolf.

(2) The hired laborer

When a hired laborer sees a wolf, he runs (vv. 12-13). He says, "This is only a job; I'm getting out of here!" He doesn't care about the sheep. When things get tough, he is gone. He is like a paid church professional who enjoys the glamour of his work. He likes collecting his checks, but when things become rough he leaves.

(3) The wolf

The worst enemy of sheep is the wolf. The hired laborer runs away, but the wolf eats the sheep. A good shepherd protects his flock, and a hired laborer abandons the flock, but the false prophet destroys the flock. They are "ravening wolves." The verb form of the Greek word for "ravening" in Matthew 7:15 literally means "to snatch or to seize." You can picture in your mind a wolf sinking his teeth into a sheep and running off with it. That same word is used in reference to a grasping extortioner in Luke 18:11 and 1 Corinthians 5:11. False prophets are ferocious, merciless, and devouring. They are extremely dangerous. That's what Jesus is saying in Matthew 7:15.

False prophets are so dangerous that we are to be wary if we are in the presence of one. Even if you associated with one and weren't influenced by him, a person with less discernment might believe you were condoning him and consequently get hurt.

*b*) Jude

The book of Jude, which talks about apostasy, says this in verse 21: "Keep yourselves in the love of God, waiting anxiously for the mercy of our Lord Jesus Christ to eternal life" (NASB). In other words, make sure you are in the place of receiving God's blessing. Make sure your life is right and that you are keeping yourself in a place where God's love is manifest. Once you have taken care of yourself, then you can win others to Christ. Verses 22-23 talk about that. There are three categories of people we can reach.

(1) The doubters

We are to "have mercy on some, who are doubting" (v. 22, NASB). When you find someone who has doubts, you are to love him and be merciful to him. That kind of person will say, "I think I believe in Christ; I think the gospel is true, but I'm not sure." Be merciful to him.

(2) The endangered unbelievers

The second group of people we are to reach out to is endangered unbelievers: "Save others, snatching them out of the fire" (v. 23, NASB). Such people are not believers; they are on their way to hell, and you have to grab them. They are indifferent outsiders.

(3) The cult members

The third category of people is those who are involved in false religions. When you reach out to them, you are to "have mercy with fear, hating even the garment polluted by the flesh" (v. 23, NASB). When you try to win a person who is under the influence of a false prophet, you have to go after him in the fear of God, or you might be influenced by that false prophet. Jude is saying that trying to win people under a false prophet's influence is dangerous because you can be defiled by him. False prophets are vile, dangerous, brute beasts. They are like lepers—you don't want to be near them.

Don't believe that false prophets are good, well-meaning, misguided people. Basically they are devouring wolves who endeavor to shove people onto the broad road to hell. Some of them may be deceiving themselves, but many of them know what they are doing.

C. The Deception

False prophets are dangerous because you don't see what they really are. Matthew 7:15 says that they "come to you in sheep's clothing, but inwardly they are ravening wolves."

1. The clothes of false prophets

   a) Imitate a true prophet's clothing

      In the Old Testament, and in the case of John the Baptist in the New Testament, a prophet was known by what he wore. Elijah, for example, wore a rough, hairy, burlap garment (2 Kings 1:8). That was a statement to society that he was forgoing comfort for the Lord's cause. John the Baptist lived in the wilderness, ate locusts and wild honey, and wore a rough camel hair coat. The camel hair products of today are not the same as they would have been then. John the Baptist's garment was uncomfortable. He wore the clothes of a prophet. God's prophets had no worldly goods and did not wear worldly clothes. They wore rough garments and came from the wilderness.

      Whenever someone wanted to pretend to be a prophet, he put on a prophet's clothing. He would wear a rough, burlap garment. Zechariah 13:4 even says that a false prophet will "wear a rough garment to deceive."

*b*) Imitate a true shepherd's clothing

When Jesus said that a false prophet wore sheep's clothing, He wasn't talking about a person's crawling on his hands and feet wearing a sheepskin. Most shepherds wore cloaks made from sheep's wool. The mark of a shepherd was his wool cloak. They needed a warm cloak because in Israel the evenings are cold. When Jesus spoke of false prophets in sheep's clothing, He was talking about people dressed like shepherds. "Sheep's clothing" is another term for wool. Just as a false prophet would wear the clothes of a prophet, a false shepherd wears the clothes of a shepherd. Jesus wasn't talking about a sheep's disguise; He was talking about a shepherd's disguise. A false shepherd looks like a shepherd, but he is really a wolf.

2. The categories of false prophets

There are three kinds of false prophets in the Bible.

*a*) The heretic

A heretic usually says, "I don't believe the Bible is true." Sometimes a heretic will say he believes the Bible but teach heretical doctrine by misusing the Bible. That kind of false prophet is openly heretical.

*b*) The apostate

Apostates deny Christianity and depart from it. They aren't hard to spot. It's easy to detect false doctrine. All you have to do is compare it with the Bible. It's easy to identify apostates—they deny the Bible.

Heretics and apostates are talked about in Matthew 7:6: "Give not that which is holy unto the dogs, neither cast your pearls before swine." It's easy to detect the hogs and dogs; they are in the mire and vomit (2 Pet. 2:22). Heretics and apostates are made obvious.

*c*) The deceiver

Deceivers the ones you have to watch out for. Jesus refers to them in Matthew 7:15. They wear the cloak of a shepherd. They talk about Jesus, the cross, God, the Scriptures, the church, and the Holy Spirit. They mingle with true Christians and appear to be evangelical. They are on the radio and television; they speak from pulpits and write books. They look like Christians. They are not as obvious as heretics. Titus 3:10 says that we are to rebuke heretics. Apostates are obvious because they have denied the faith. But deceivers are subtle.

The Lord is not warning us about heretics or apostates in Matthew 7:15. He is warning us about people who sound like Christians and appear to teach the gospel. We shouldn't be surprised that there will be people like that. Second Corinthians 11:14 says, "Satan himself is transformed into an angel of light." He is hidden among us. Verse 15 says, "Therefore, it is no great thing if his ministers also be transformed as the ministers of righteousness." They are subtle deceivers in our midst. Jude 4 says, "There are certain men crept in unawares." They are everywhere.

3. The characteristics of false prophets

Sometimes when I point out a false prophet with the help of the Word and Spirit of God, other Christians become upset. They say, "That person a deceiver? Impossible!" But all the criteria need to be examined.

*a*) Their words

False prophets are pleasant. They mingle with Christians and talk like Christians. It's not what false prophets say, however, that gives them away; it's what they don't say. They talk about Jesus, the cross, and heaven, but they never talk about sin, hell, mourning, meekness, and humility. They only talk about how to be happy.

*b)* Their ways

False prophets appear to live righteous lives. You may say, "If someone is a false prophet, his life wouldn't be clean." Some of them live superficially clean lives, but deep inside they are rotten. Commentator John A. Broadus said, "When some teachers of ruinous heresy are men of scrupulous conduct and pleasing general character, and even very devout, this may usually be ascribed to their religious education and early habits" (*Commentary on the Gospel of Matthew* [Valley Forge, Pa.: Judson, 1886], p. 167).

False prophets appear to walk the Christian walk. They may appear to be fine, but they are vile on the inside. They suppress their depravity for the sake of their reputation. Sometimes when such a person's sin is revealed, the people in his church say, "We are supposed to be forgiving," and the false prophet continues in his sinfulness.

False prophets are deceptive. Beware, for deceivers are all around us. They are not as obvious as heretics and apostates; they appear to be Christians.

D. The Damnation

1. The conversation detailed

False prophets will have an end. According to Matthew 7:22, they will say to Jesus at the time of judgment, "Lord, Lord, have we not prophesied in thy name?" In other words, they will say, "We were Your preachers."

## Prophets of Revelation and Prophets of Proclamation

The false prophets mentioned in Matthew 7 were not the kind of prophets that received revelation from God. There were Old and New Testament prophets that God spoke through directly, but not all prophets received direct revelation. The word *prophesy* means "to speak before." That's why the gift of prophecy still exists: it is not just a revelatory gift; it is nonrevelatory also. A prophet is one

The false prophets in Matthew 7:22 will claim to have prophesied in Christ's name. Some of them might say they received revelations from God, but basically they will claim to have declared Christ's name. The Lord will say to them, "I never knew you; depart from me, ye that work iniquity" (v. 23). Christ will send false prophets into everlasting damnation.

2. The condemnation detailed

   a) They will not be alone

   The great tragedy is that the false prophets won't go to hell alone, for "many there be who go in that way" (Matt. 7:13). Second Peter 2:2 says that "many shall follow their pernicious ways." A great number of people will be deceived, and their end will be eternal destruction. Second Peter 2:1 says, "There were false prophets also among the people, even as there shall be false teachers among you, who secretly shall bring in destructive heresies, even denying the Lord that bought them, and bring upon themselves swift destruction." They are not alone; many will follow them to the same fate.

   b) They will not be spared

   Second Peter 2:4-6 says, "God spared not the angels that sinned, but cast them down to hell . . . and spared not the old world, but saved Noah . . . and [turned] the cities of Sodom and Gomorrah into ashes." If God did all that, then He will not spare false prophets. Verse 9 says that He will "reserve the unjust unto the day of judgment to be punished." False prophets will "utterly perish in their own corruption" (v. 12). They are cursed children (v. 14), for "whom the mist of darkness is reserved forever" (v. 17). In Revelation 19:20, we read that the false prophet of the Antichrist and the Antichrist himself will be thrown into the lake of fire, which will burn forever.

Christ has warned us. The first word in Matthew 7:15 is "beware." We have examined the definition, the danger, the deception, and the damnation of false prophets. Be on the lookout: they are dangerous because they are deceptive —and their deception leads to damnation.

In our next lesson, we will learn more about how to recognize them. It is important for us to be able to separate the true from the false. Too many Christians today are vague about doctrine and gullible regarding anyone who talks about Jesus. There are many false prophets around us. We need to understand how to determine who is of God and who is not.

### Focusing on the Facts

1. Jesus invited men to come to Him at the end of His Sermon on the Mount (Matt. 7:13-14). What other invitations did Jesus make in the New Testament (see pp. 30-31)?
2. Explain what is said in the invitation in Isaiah 55:1 (see p. 31).
3. What is happening in Matthew 23:37? Why (see p. 32)?
4. What is one reason that it is difficult to enter the narrow gate (see pp. 32-33)?
5. What did God want Israel to do with a false prophet according to Deuteronomy 13:1-5 (see pp. 33-34)?
6. What do the Israelites ask the prophets to do in Isaiah 30:10? Why (see p. 34)?
7. What does Romans 16:17-18 say about false prophets (see pp. 34-35)?
8. What two things was a true prophet known by (see p. 35)?
9. What does God say about false prophets in Jeremiah 23:14-16 (see pp. 36-37)?
10. List some terms that are used in the New Testament to speak of false prophets (see p. 38).
11. How do we know that false prophets will always have an audience? Use Scripture to support your answer (see p. 38).
12. What does the Greek word for "beware" in Matthew 7:15 mean? Why should we not pay attention to false prophets (see pp. 38-39)?
13. What terms do Peter and Jude use to describe false prophets (see p. 39)?

14. What does a good shepherd do when a wolf threatens his sheep (see p. 40)?
15. What does a hired laborer do when the sheep under his care are threatened by a wolf? What kind of church worker does he depict (see p. 40)?
16. What does a wolf (false prophet) do to sheep (see p. 40)?
17. How are we to reach out to doubters? How do we need to reach out to endangered unbelievers? Why must we be so cautious when reaching out to those who are under the influence of a false prophet (Jude 22-23; see pp. 41-42)?
18. What did a person do if he wanted to pretend to be a prophet? What Scripture verse supports that (see p. 42)?
19. Explain what Jesus meant when He said that a false prophet wore sheep's clothing (see p. 43).
20. What three categories of false prophets are there? How can a person detect false prophets from the first two categories? Why is it so difficult to spot false prophets from the third category (see pp. 43-44)?
21. Of the three categories of false prophets, what category is Jesus referring to in Matthew 7:15 (see p. 44)?
22. Describe the words and the ways of a false prophet (see pp. 44-45).
23. What appeal will false prophets make to Christ at judgment? What will Christ's answer be (Matt. 7:22-23; see pp. 45-46)?
24. What is the great tragedy about the condemnation of false prophets (see p. 46)?
25. How do we know that God will not spare false prophets? Support your answer with Scripture (see pp. 46-47).

### Pondering the Principles

1. There are many people today who misunderstand what the Bible teaches because they have been exposed to a false prophet. Would you be able to explain to such people what the Scriptures really teach? If not, take time now to write down some common misunderstandings people have about God, Christ, salvation, and other major themes in the Bible. During this week, with the help of a Bible, good Christian books, or other Christians, learn how to refute those misconceptions. Write what you learn in a notebook, and keep adding information as you learn more about those things. As a representative of Christ, you must "study to show thyself approved unto God, a workman that

needeth not to be ashamed, rightly dividing the word of truth"
(2 Tim. 2:15).

2. In Acts 20:29 Paul tells the elders of the church at Ephesus, "For
I know this, that after my departing shall grievous wolves enter
in among you, not sparing the flock." Jesus warned us to "beware of false prophets . . . in sheep's clothing" (Matt. 7:15). Although Christians must be careful not to be influenced by false
prophets, they do not need to fear falling prey to false teaching
and losing their salvation. Read the following passages and
write down the promises given in them: Psalms 23:4-5; 121;
John 10:28; Romans 5:1-11; 8:38-39; Hebrews 13:5b-6; 1 Peter 1:3-
5; 1 John 5:11-13; and Jude 24. Summarize in your own words
the protection that the Lord provides for us. Thank Him for that
protection.

# 3
# Beware of False Prophets—Part 2

### Outline

Introduction
A. The Tragic Commentary of a False Prophet
B. The Three Categories of False Prophets
  1. The heretics
  2. The apostates
  3. The deceivers

Review
I. Warning
  A. The Definition
  B. The Danger
    1. Declared
    2. Defined
    3. Depicted
    4. Destroyed
      *a*) By comparison
      *b*) By consecration
  C. The Deception
  D. The Damnation

Lesson
II. Watching
  A. The Measure of False Prophets
    1. The passages
    2. The precaution
    3. The principle
  B. The Makeup of False Prophets

1. Their character
   a) Actions
      (1) Of true believers
          (a) Their occurrence
          (b) Their origin
      (2) Of false prophets
          (a) The internal reality
          (b) The external image
   b) Attitudes
      (1) The contrast
      (2) The criterion
          (a) The traits to analyze
          (b) The test to apply
2. Their creed
   a) Discerned
   b) Described
      (1) Their doctrinal error
      (2) Their deceitful evangelism
          (a) Discussed by Martin Lloyd-Jones
          (b) Discussed by Arthur Pink
3. Their converts
4. Their condemnation

Conclusion
A. The Peril
   1. The ways of false prophets
   2. The words of false prophets
B. The Protection

## Introduction

Matthew 7:15-20 says, "Beware of false prophets, who come to you in sheep's clothing, but inwardly they are ravening wolves. Ye shall know them by their fruits. Do men gather grapes of thorns, or figs of thistles? Even so, every good tree bringeth forth good fruit, but a corrupt tree bringeth forth bad fruit. A good tree cannot bring forth bad fruit, neither can a corrupt tree bring forth good fruit. Every tree that bringeth not forth good fruit is hewn down, and cast into the fire. Wherefore, by their fruits ye shall know them." The emphasis of that text is in the first few words: "Beware of false prophets."

A. The Tragic Commentary of a False Prophet

In our lifetime occurred the incredible tragedy known as Jonestown. If anyone needs an illustration of a false prophet, Jim Jones is the person to look at. In him we see the character, teaching, life-style, and approach of a false prophet. Unfortunately, not all false prophets are so obvious. That's why Hebrews 5:14 talks about the need to have our "senses exercised to discern both good and evil." False prophets aren't always patently obvious.

The greatest tragedy of Jonestown is not that nearly a thousand people died. Everyone will one day die. The tragedy is that most of them died and went to hell believing that they were serving God and were on their way to heaven. It's sad that they had untimely deaths, but it's even more sad that they are in timeless eternity. Jim Jones fooled people into believing that he represented God and Christ. His followers believed that they were serving the kingdom of God, but many of them are in hell now. Satan is a liar and deceiver, as are his emissaries, who masquerade as angels of light (2 Cor. 11:14-15).

Jim Jones wasn't the only false prophet. Jesus said, "For there shall arise false Christs, and false prophets, and shall show great signs and wonders, insomuch that, if it were possible, they shall deceive the very elect" (Matt. 24:24). Jude wrote, "There are certain men crept in unawares . . . turning the grace of our God into lasciviousness" (v. 4). False prophets will always be around. Jim Jones was only one of them. Not all false prophets are like Jim Jones in their way of operating. He reached the poor; other false prophets reach the middle class and the rich. Jim Jones practiced blatant, flagrant authoritarianism; some false prophets are more subtle. He was outwardly vile; others appear virtuous. False prophets come in all kinds of packages. However, their hearts are always the same. They have the heart of the devil.

B. The Three Categories of False Prophets

There are three kinds of false prophets.

1. The heretics

   Heretics openly defy the truth. Paul said that they should be admonished and put away (Titus 3:10). Heretics pit themselves against the Bible. They are flagrant and don't fool anyone.

2. The apostates

   Apostates know the truth but turn their backs on it. They too are flagrantly against the truth.

3. The deceivers

   I call obscure false prophets the deceivers. They never openly admit that they are against the truth. They will not accept the fact that they are heretics or apostates. Deceivers are wolves wearing a shepherd's garments. As Jude 4 says, they creep among us when we're not aware. Some of them may be found out in the end, as was Jim Jones. They stand at the crossroads where people make a choice between the narrow gate that leads to life and the broad gate that leads to destruction. Although the Spirit of God calls people to the narrow gate, false prophets shove them onto the broad way that leads to hell. The deceivers vary in how sophisticated they are, and they have different levels of education. They wear all kinds of clothes and ecclesiastical trappings, but they are all the same.

   When the Lord said "Beware of false prophets," He had the Pharisees and scribes in mind. He saw them as false prophets. They acted religious and tried to keep every minute aspect of the law. The scruples they maintained for their religion were beyond imagination. They assumed that their religiosity would put them in the highest level of the kingdom of God. Yet Jesus called them false prophets. Someone once said, "You can dot all your i's and cross all your t's and not spell the word right." In a sense, the Pharisees and scribes kept all the jots and tittles of the law but didn't spell Jesus. They were acting religious, yet they damned their followers to hell.

Jesus was saying, "In your effort to enter the narrow gate that leads to life, beware of the emissaries of Satan. They will try to deceive you." False prophets aren't at the crossroads saying, "Hey, everybody, let's go to hell!" They are saying, "This is the way to heaven."

Two words head our outline for Matthew 7:15-20: *warning* and *watching*.

## Review

I. WARNING (see pp. 33-47)

Men and women all over the world are standing at the crossroads before the narrow gate and the wide gate. False prophets stand there trying to deceive them. Believers need to preach the truth; we must warn people about false prophets.

A. The Definition (see pp. 35-38)

The Greek word for "prophets" is *prophētēs*, which means "those who speak forth or speak before." Both true and false prophets are found in the Old Testament. True prophets were known by two things: they had a divine commission and a divine message. They spoke for and from God. False prophets didn't have a divine commission or a divine message. They stood on their own authority and spoke their own false messages. False prophets were addressed by the Greek words *pseudoprophētēs* ("false prophets," Matt. 24:11), *pseudochristos* ("false Christs," Matt. 24:24), and *pseudoadelphos* ("false brethren," 2 Cor. 11:26). The Greek prefix *pseudo* means "false."

B. The Danger

Verse 15 starts with the word *beware*, which in this context means "to hold your mind back from." In other words, don't expose yourself to false prophets. Jude 23 says that if you try to reach out to people under the influence of a false prophet, do it with fear, because that false prophet could subtly influence you.

1. Declared (see pp. 38-39)

2. Defined (see pp. 39-42)

3. Depicted

   Second John 7 illustrates the danger of false prophets: "For many deceivers are entered into the world, who confess not that Jesus Christ cometh in the flesh [i.e., they do not hold a biblical view of who He is and what He did]." What are you to do if you meet such a person? Recognize that "this is a deceiver and an antichrist." Verse 8 continues, "Look to yourselves [examine yourselves], that we lose not those things which we have wrought, but that we receive a full reward." In other words, if you are deceived by a false prophet, you won't lose your salvation, but you will forfeit the reward you've already earned by your service to Christ. Verse 10 says, "If there come any unto you, and bring not this doctrine [the doctrine of Christ, v. 9], receive him not into your house, neither bid him Godspeed." Don't expose yourself to false prophets, and don't wish them well. They are so wretched and deceitful that you shouldn't even welcome them. You can deal with a heretic or an apostate, but you can't deal with a deceiver without getting stained by his filthiness.

4. Destroyed

   What is your protection against that danger?

   a) By comparison

      Concerning false prophets 2 Timothy 3:8 says, "Now as Jannes and Jambres withstood Moses [they were false prophets in Moses' time], so do these also resist the truth, men of corrupt minds, reprobate concerning the faith." What are we to do about those evil men? We must recognize that they will be judged (v. 9). They don't believe what we believe. Then Paul says to Timothy, "Thou hast fully known my doctrine, manner of life, purpose, faith, long-suffering, love, [and] patience" (v. 10). Paul was saying, "you know that I am different from false prophets. You know how to distinguish between them and those who are right." Paul then said, "Evil men and seducers shall become worse and worse, deceiving, and being deceived" (v. 13). Some false prophets are deceived themselves. Someone once asked me, "Do you believe false prophets know they are false prophets?" Some do, and some don't. They continue in satanic delusion and draw others into it.

*b)* By consecration

In 2 Timothy 3:14-17 Paul says more about how to protect yourself against false prophets. You must hold your mind back from them. However, your mind cannot be in a vacuum. You've got to put something in it: "Continue thou in the things which thou hast learned and hast been assured of, knowing of whom thou hast learned them" (v. 14). Remember godly people and what you've learned from them. Paul says to Timothy in verse 15, "From [when you were] a child thou hast known the holy scriptures, which are able to make thee wise unto salvation through faith which is in Christ Jesus." Verses 16-17 continue, "All scripture is given by inspiration of God . . . that the man of God may be perfect, thoroughly furnished unto all good works." Give yourself to studying Scripture. Hold your mind back from false prophets, and fill it with the Word of God. Have your mind on God (Isa. 26:3). Peter said, "Gird up the loins of your mind" (1 Pet. 1:13). Keep your mind on God and the Scriptures, because if you don't, a wolf in shepherd's clothing will tear you apart in a ferocious, devouring manner.

C. The Deception (see pp. 42-45)

False prophets wear sheep's clothing (the wool garment that a shepherd wears). You may believe you can spot them, but you're going to have to look carefully. They aren't outwardly recognizable. Many Christian leaders work with them for common causes. False prophets are deceitful.

D. The Damnation (see pp. 45-47)

Jude 13 says that false prophets will be condemned to "the blackness of darkness forever." The Lord will say to them and their followers, "I never knew you; depart from me, ye that work iniquity" (Matt. 7:23).

**Lesson**

## II. WATCHING

Let me say something that is important in this day of compromise: many false prophets today are claiming to be Christians, and many true believers are linking arms with them. Since we have been warned, what do we watch for? How do we recognize false prophets? What are their characteristics?

A. The Measure of False Prophets

1. The passages

God didn't just instruct us to beware of false prophets; He helps us recognize them. Because they are dangerous, He helps us understand what to look for. Matthew 7:16 says, "Ye shall know them by their fruits." That is not a command; it is an assurance. Verse 20 says, "Wherefore, by their fruits ye shall know them."

2. The precaution

There is an old proverb that says, "Like fruit, like root." The Jews, Greeks, and Romans all said that a tree is judged by its fruit. If you want to know whether a prophet is true or false, look at what he produces. Be careful: just because a person is associated with Christians doesn't mean that he can't be a false prophet. Christians are deceived by false prophets. Matthew 7:16 identifies them as grapes stuck on thorns and figs stuck on thistles. Grapes don't grow on thorns, and figs don't grow on thistles, but you can stick them on. Only close examination will reveal that a thorn didn't produce a grape and a thistle didn't produce a fig. There are Christians who unwittingly attach themselves to a false teacher who appears to be a Christian.

3. The principle

A simple principle is presented to us in verses 17 and 18: good trees make good fruit, and bad trees make bad fruit. That is simple. A bad tree will have bad fruit and bad sap. That doesn't mean the tree and its fruit will look wretched and shriveled. A good tree and a bad tree may look alike. It's not until you taste the fruit that you are going to be able to distinguish between them. It's easy to be deceived. That's why when God evaluates men, He looks at their hearts, not their outward appearance (1 Sam. 16:7).

When you look at a false prophet, you might see real fruit attached to him, but it's only stuck on a thorn or a thistle. The fruit that he really produces is going to be bad—no matter what it looks like on the outside.

B. The Makeup of False Prophets

What are you looking for when you examine a person's fruit? There are four things to look for in false prophets.

1. Their character

When you examine the life of a person who might be a false prophet, ask yourself these questions: What kind of character does he have? What is his personality like? What are his attitudes and actions like? Look at his motives, thoughts, and perspective toward life. Examine his life-style. Watch how he thinks and acts. Character is the first element that manifests fruit. The Bible confirms that.

*a*) Actions

(1) Of true believers

(*a*) Their occurrence

In Luke 3:8 John the Baptist says to a group of scribes and Pharisees, "Bring forth, therefore, fruits worthy of repentance." He was saying, "You say that you have repented and committed yourselves to God. Let's see the fruit." Verses 10-13 say, "And the people asked him, saying, What shall we do, then? He answereth, and saith unto them, He that hath two coats, let him impart to him that hath none; and he that hath food, let him do the same. Then came also tax collectors to be baptized, and said unto him, Teacher, what shall we do? And he said unto them, Exact no more than that which is appointed you." John the Baptist was telling those people that the fruit of repentance included giving to someone in need and not taking more than you deserve. Fruit is an action; it is a life-style. Some people believe that the fruit in that passage is manifest in doctrine, but it is really manifest in action.

Another example of fruit manifest through action appears in John 15:8. Jesus said, "In this is my Father glorified, that ye bear much fruit." How do we bear fruit? By keeping God's commandments (v. 10). Fruit is obedience; it is action in response to God's commands.

(*b*) Their origin

Fruit is not only your actions but also the attitudes behind your actions. Galatians 5:22-23 says that "the fruit of the Spirit is love, joy, peace, long-suffering, gentleness, goodness, faith, meekness, [and] self-control." Ephesians 5:9-12 talks about the fruit of light. It is the light of God in your heart that produces certain kinds of attitudes. Philippians 1:11 refers to our actions and attitudes as "the fruits of righteousness." Colossians 1:10 talks about "being fruitful in every good work." Fruit includes both actions and attitudes.

The first test of a false prophet is his character. Watch his actions. True righteousness can't come from a rotten tree. Check a person's life-style, because whatever is in his heart will come out (Luke 6:45).

(2) Of false prophets

(a) The internal reality

Speaking of false prophets, Peter said, "Spots they are and blemishes, reveling with their own deceivings while they feast with you; having eyes full of adultery" (2 Pet. 2:13-14). They go after their lusts all the time. Peter also called them covetous, cursed children (v. 14). They hunger for money. They are lascivious, brute beasts.

(b) The external image

False prophets won't always look like that outwardly. They can cover themselves with ecclesiastical robes and a supposedly Christian life-style. They make themselves look good by belonging to Christian organizations, working with Christian leaders, and talking about the Bible, Jesus, and salvation. False prophets hide the truth about their moral lives. A person may appear to be living out the gospel when in reality he isn't. Sometimes you can't detect a false prophet by his actions. The Pharisees looked good. They didn't openly murder and commit adultery. They fasted, prayed, and tithed. They appeared to live good lives. But if you examine false prophets carefully, you'll find many skeletons in their moral closets. There will be wretchedness, greed, or immorality in their lives.

*b)* Attitudes

Often false prophets can suppress their vileness. Their evil may not be obvious by their actions. That's when you need to take note of the way they think and their attitudes.

(1) The contrast

Second Peter contrasts the attitudes of true believers with false prophets. True believers are "partakers of the divine nature, having escaped the corruption that is in the world through lust" (1:4). A true believer has received the very nature of God and has escaped corruption. In other words, he is not rotting internally. However, 2 Peter 2:19 says of false prophets: "While they promise them liberty, they themselves are the servants of corruption." They have not escaped corruption. However, verse 20 says, "They have escaped the pollutions of the world." Peter is differentiating between internal corruption and external pollution. He is saying that false prophets have never changed on the inside, but they have washed off the ashes of the world externally. Many false prophets deal with the pollution on the outside. They look good temporarily; their actions appear right. You can't find any moral skeletons in their closets. If that is the case, you need to go beyond their external actions to their corrupt internal attitudes. Try to find motives behind what they do.

(2) The criterion

It is important for you to check out suspect prophets not only for your sake but for the sake of the people who are trapped in their evil systems. If a person's motives do not include a desire to glorify God, magnify Christ, live holily, overcome sin, be humble, and be selfless, then all of his goodness is "as filthy rags [menstrual cloths]" (Isa. 64:6). If a person appears washed on the outside, check what he is like on the inside. Jesus said to the Pharisees and scribes, "Ye are like whited sepulchers, which indeed appear beautiful outward, but are within full of dead men's bones, and of all uncleanness" (Matt. 23:27). In the Sermon on the Mount Jesus tries to communicate that what is inside is what counts. The Pharisees had managed to get the pollution off on the outside, but they still needed to deal with what was inside.

(a) The traits to analyze

When you examine a false prophet, check for the presence of a Beatitude attitude. That's the evidence of internal transformation. Is he poor in spirit and meek (Matt. 5:3, 5)? Does he mourn over his sins (Matt. 5:4)? Does he hunger and thirst for righteousness and long for mercy (Matt. 5:6-7)? Is he a peacemaker and willing to be persecuted for the sake of Christ (Matt. 5:9-10)? False prophets are absorbed with pride, power, prestige, and promotion. They want to be famous and loved, not persecuted. Second Peter 2:3 says they are involved in religion for money: "Through covetousness shall they, with feigned words, make merchandise of you." Second Corinthians 2:17 says that false prophets are hucksters of the Word. They are not sincere. Such people sell Jesus as though He were cheap glass, not a diamond. They're involved with religion and prestige. Second Peter 2 says, "Presumptuous are they; self-willed, they are not afraid to speak evil of dignities. . . . They speak great swelling words of vanity" (vv. 10, 18).

False prophets are self-centered, proud, jealous of others, and impure. You won't find a shred of humility in them. They don't mourn over their sin or stand meek before God. They don't have the same fear before God that Paul had.

Commentator Martin Lloyd-Jones said, "A Christian can generally be known by his very appearance. The man who really believes in the holiness of God, and who knows his own sinfulness and the blackness of his own heart, the man who believes in the judgment of God and the possibility of hell and torment, the man who really believes that he himself is so vile and helpless that nothing but the coming of the Son of God from heaven to earth, and His going to the bitter shame and agony and cruelty of the cross could ever save him, and reconcile him to God—this man is going to show all that in his whole personality. He is a man who is bound to give the impression of meekness. He is bound to be humble. Our Lord reminds us here that if a man is not humble, we are to be very wary of him. He can put on a kind of sheep's clothing, but that is not true humility, that is not true meekness. And if a man's doctrine is wrong, it will generally show itself at this point. He will be affable and pleasant, he will appeal to the natural man, and to the things that are physical and carnal; but he will not give the impression of being a man who has seen himself as a hell-bound sinner, and who has been saved by the grace of God alone" (*Studies in the Sermon on the Mount* [Grand Rapids: Eerdmans, 1977], pp. 258-59).

(*b*) The test to apply

False prophets attract both unbelievers and believers. They appeal to the natural man and look good. Scrutinize their lives carefully. If you can't distinguish them by their actions, look for humility. Jesus said, "He that speaketh of himself seeketh his own glory" (John 7:18). He also said, "I seek not mine own will, but the will of the Father who hath sent me" (John 5:30). If Jesus applied that standard to Himself, we can use that test against any man. John Calvin said, "Nothing is more difficult than to counterfeit virtue" (*Calvin's Commentaries: The Gospels* [Grand Rapids: Assoc. Pub. and Authors, n.d.], p. 160). You'll find the truth if you look.

2. Their creed

A creed refers to the teaching of a person. A false prophet's teaching will be wrong. He will also subtly leave certain things out of what he teaches. What he says might sound good because it's what he doesn't say that's really important. Matthew 12 says, "Either make the tree good, and its fruit good, or else make the tree corrupt, and its fruit corrupt; for the tree is known by its fruit. O generation of vipers, how can ye, being evil, speak good things? For out of the abundance of the heart the mouth speaketh. . . . For by thy words thou shalt be justified, and by thy words thou shalt be condemned" (vv. 33-34, 37).

*a*) Discerned

Listen carefully to what a person is saying. Does he speak from the Bible? Does he give the whole counsel of God from beginning to end? Can he say with Paul, "Wherefore, I testify unto you this day, that I am pure from the blood of all men; for I have not shunned to declare unto you all the counsel of God" (Acts 20:26-27)? Isaiah 8:20 says, "To the law and to the testimony; if they speak not according to this word, it is because there is no light in them." You show me a man who does not teach from God's Word, and I'll show you a false prophet. Sometimes false prophets talk about the Bible but not from it. They can't expose their lives to the light of the Word.

If a man doesn't teach what Scripture teaches, he is a false prophet. Compare what a person teaches with the Bible, and watch out for what he doesn't say.

*b*) Described

You can always detect false prophets because they have a twisted view of Christ's Person and work. What was Christ's work? Salvation. When you deal with a false prophet, look at what he teaches about salvation, because that's the issue every false prophet mixes up.

(1) Their doctrinal error

The Lord said that it's not easy to become saved. He said that you must go through "the narrow gate" (Matt. 7:13). At the end of verse 14 He says, "Few there be that find it." You must agonize to enter the gate—it is a hard way. However, a false prophet doesn't teach that. His doctrine of salvation says that the way to heaven is broad and that everyone can come. He says, "All you have to do is believe in Jesus." He talks about Christ's death and resurrection and sounds like he is preaching the gospel. But he says that everyone can enter heaven easily.

Commentator Arthur Pink said, "False prophets . . . are to be found in the circles of the most orthodox and pretend to have a fervent love for souls, yet they fatally delude multitudes concerning the way of salvation. . . . The pulpit, platform, pamphlet hucksters [I'm sure he would have added radio and TV if he were alive today] have so wantonly lowered the standard of divine holiness and so adulterated the Gospel in order to make it palatable to the carnal mind" (*An Exposition of the Sermon on the Mount* [Grand Rapids: Baker, 1953]).

False prophets have a cheap doctrine of salvation. They say that a person can become saved by signing a card, walking an aisle, raising his hand, or loving Jesus. They say it doesn't matter what your life is like.

## (2) Their deceitful evangelism

False prophets do not teach that there is a narrow gate. The deception is in what they don't say. They don't want to offend anyone. Their message is comforting and happy. They are praised by liberals and sometimes even by evangelicals. False prophets may present Christ as "the way, the truth, and the life" (John 14:6), but they won't say anything about the narrow gate. They teach an easy salvation: all a person needs to do is come down an aisle and get baptized. Their message emphasizes health, happiness, and positive thinking. They are compromisers.

False prophets say everything is fine when that's not true. They don't talk about repentance, judgment, brokenness, a contrite heart, or deep sorrow over sin. Their words are comforting, positive, and loving. That's why people flock to them: they like happy, Holy Spirit healers, positive thinkers, and cheap grace preachers. Those men say "peace, peace" when there is no peace (Jer. 6:14).

### (a) Discussed by Martin Lloyd-Jones

Martin Lloyd-Jones was correct when he said that false prophets are characterized by an almost entire absence of doctrine. They don't want to talk about doctrine or theology. Everything they say is vague and ethereal. False prophets don't speak about holiness, obedience, righteousness, justice, and judgment. They focus on happiness, health, positive thinking, and easy believism. They please people all the way to hell; there is never a call for repentance. Martin Lloyd-Jones said that is unlike the evangelism of John Wesley, George Whitefield, and the Puritans. He said, "John Bunyan tells us in his *Grace Abounding* that he endured an agony of repentance for eighteen months. There does not seem to be much room for that today. Repentance means that you realize that you are a guilty, vile sinner in the presence of God, that you are hell-bound. It means that you begin to realize that this thing called sin is in you, that you long to get rid of it, and that you turn your back on it in every shape and form. You renounce the world whatever the cost, the world in its mind and outlook as well as its practice, and you deny yourself, and take up the cross and go after Christ. Your nearest and dearest, and the whole world, may call you a fool, or say you have religious mania. You may have to suffer financially, but it makes no difference. That is repentance" (*Studies in the Sermon on the Mount* [Grand Rapids: Eerdmans, 1977]).

False prophets don't preach like that. They are vague about everything. We had better listen to the true prophets and not the false!

(*b*) Discussed by Arthur Pink

Arthur Pink said, "Certain it is, my reader, that any preacher who rejects God's Law, who denies repentance to be a condition of salvation, who assures the giddy and godless that they are loved by God, who declares that saving faith is nothing more than an act of the will which every person has the power to perform, is a false prophet, and should be shunned as a deadly plague" (*An Exposition of the Sermon on the Mount* [Grand Rapids: Baker, 1953]).

How can you detect false prophets? By their fruits. Look at their character and creed.

3. Their converts

When you want to learn more about a leader, look at the lives of his followers. Peter said, "Many shall follow their pernicious ways" (2 Pet. 2:2). Part of a leader's fruit is his converts. Paul called converts "fruit" in Romans 1:13. Look at the people following a leader and accepting his influence. Do you see humility and thirsting for righteousness? Or are they on the Jesus bandwagon? Do you see real virtue and godliness in them?

4. Their condemnation

Matthew 7:19 says, "Every tree that bringeth not forth good fruit is hewn down, and cast into the fire." Ultimately you can tell a false prophet by his condemnation.

## Why Has God Allowed False Prophets to Exist?

God has ordained that false prophets exist. I used to wonder why He allowed that until I learned the answer from Scripture. First Corinthians 11:19 says, "For there must be also heresies among you." You may ask, "Why does the Lord allow heresies? Why does the Lord allow false prophets to trouble us?" The end of 1 Corinthians 11:19 gives the answer: "[In order] that they who are approved may be made manifest among you." In other words, heresy is a magnet that draws false disciples and leaves manifest true ones. It's like a wind that blows the chaff away. Error separates the chaff and the wheat. With the existence of both true and false prophets, God reveals who is genuine. It's true that some true believers associate with false prophets and that there are unbelievers sown among believers (Matt. 13:25). But generally, false prophets are ordained by God to draw ungodly people to themselves. They damn those who follow them. That's part of God's judgment.

Second Thessalonians 2:11-12 says, "For this cause God shall send them strong delusion, that they should believe the lie, that they all might be judged who believed not the truth." God allows delusion because it attracts those who reject Christ—it separates them from the wheat. False prophets are ordained for judgment.

### Conclusion

A. The Peril

1. The ways of false prophets

We've seen the warning. Watch out for false prophets. Many of them will look like true believers. They will be pleasant, sincere people who talk about Jesus, the Bible, and salvation. They will be inoffensive, accommodating to other people's viewpoints, rarely criticized by others, and praised by many. Large crowds will listen to them and believe they are great. It is those people that the false prophets shove onto the broad way that leads to destruction.

2. The words of false prophets

Listen carefully, because false prophets don't talk about a narrow way. They talk about God's love, not His wrath. They talk about people being deprived, not depraved. Their message is about God as the loving, understanding Father of everyone. Nothing is said about a holy God whose only children are those of faith in Christ. Their message has gaps; they leave out the truth that saves.

B. The Protection

I want to conclude with Paul's warning to the Ephesian elders in the book of Acts: "For I know this, that after my departing shall grievous wolves enter in among you, not sparing the flock. Also of your own selves shall men arise, speaking perverse things, to draw away disciples after them. Therefore, watch, and remember, that for the space of three years I ceased not to warn everyone night and day with tears" (20:29-31). The words *watch* and *warn* appear there. Paul told them, "I've warned you; watch out for those wolves! They will be in your midst." Then Paul says in verse 32, "And now, brethren, I commend you . . . to the word of his grace." God's Word is our protection.

### Focusing on the Facts

1. What is most tragic about what happened at Jonestown (see p. 53)?
2. According to 2 John 7, what is a false prophet? Will you lose your salvation if you are deceived by a false prophet (2 John 8)? Explain (see p. 56).

3. What should our response be to false prophets who visit us (2 John 10; see p. 56)?
4. How can we protect ourselves from false prophets? Use 2 Timothy 3:8-9, 14-17 to support your answer (see pp. 56-57).
5. How does Matthew 7:16 identify Christians who are deceived by false prophets (see pp. 56-57)?
6. How can we recognize false prophets (Matt. 7:16, 20; see p. 58)?
7. How does one distinguish between a good tree and a bad tree (see p. 59)?
8. What did John the Baptist mean when he said to a group of scribes and Pharisees, "Bring forth, therefore, fruits worthy of repentance" (Luke 3:8; see pp. 59-60)?
9. How do Christians bear fruit (John 15:10; see p. 60)?
10. Fruit is not only your _____ but also the _____ behind them (see p. 60).
11. Describe the internal reality and external image of a false prophet (see p. 61).
12. If you can't find anything wrong with the actions of a false prophet, what should you examine next (see p. 61)?
13. What does 2 Peter 1:4 say about true believers? What does 2 Peter 2:19 say about false prophets (see p. 62)?
14. What is Peter differentiating between when he says false prophets "are the servants of corruption," yet "they have escaped the pollutions of the world"? Explain (2 Pet. 2:19-20; see p. 62).
15. When trying to discern a false prophet, check for the presence of a Beatitude attitude. What are the characteristics of that attitude (see p. 63)?
16. What characterizes a false prophet's teaching (see p. 63)?
17. What did Jesus teach about salvation? What do false prophets teach about salvation (see p. 66)?
18. What did Martin Lloyd-Jones say false prophets are characterized by? What things do false prophets not talk about? What do they focus on (see p. 67)?
19. When evaluating whether a person is a false prophet, why would looking at his converts be helpful (see p. 68)?
20. Explain why God allows false prophets to exist. Support your answer with Scripture (see p. 69).
21. What does Paul say in his warning to the Ephesian elders in Acts 20:29-31? What protects us from the danger of which Paul spoke (v. 32; see p. 70)?

# Pondering the Principles

1. When you listen to someone who professes to teach the Bible, examine him carefully. Just because his teaching sounds good to you doesn't mean that he is a true Christian. Paul used himself as an example for Timothy to compare with other teachers: "Thou hast fully known my doctrine, manner of life, purpose, faith, long-suffering, love, [and] patience" (2 Tim. 3:10). If you had to examine a person right now to find out whether or not he is a false prophet, what specific things would you look for? List them. Now list the things you would look for to prove that a person is a Christian. Compare your two lists, and summarize what you have learned from them.

2. A false prophet's teaching is both wrong and incomplete. Read Romans 16:17-18. Whom should we avoid? How do false teachers "deceive the hearts of the innocent" (v. 18)? Who does Paul say should be accursed in Galatians 1:8-9? Read Ephesians 4:14. By what should we not be "tossed to and fro"? Using what you have just learned, explain why it is so important to know what the Bible teaches.

# 4
# Empty Words and Empty Hearts—Part 1

## Outline

Introduction
A. Entrance into Heaven Through Christ's Righteousness
   1. The conditions stipulated
   2. The choices stated
   3. The complications specified
      a) You must find it
      b) You must leave the crowd
      c) You must enter unencumbered
      d) You must enter repentantly
      e) You must beware of false prophets
B. Exclusion from Heaven by Self-Deception
   1. The categories of self-deception
   2. The caution about self-deception
      a) Emphasized
      b) Exemplified
   3. The causes of self-deception
      a) A false doctrine of assurance
         (1) The inadequacy of human assurance
         (2) The importance of divine assurance
      b) A failure to examine yourself
      c) A fixation on religious activity
      d) A fair-exchange approach
   4. The characteristics of self-deception

Lesson
I. The Folly of Empty Words (vv. 21-23)
   A. The Conversation
      1. The remarks of the self-deceived
         a) "Lord, Lord"
         b) "In thy name"

## Introduction

A. Entrance into Heaven Through Christ's Righteousness

1. The conditions stipulated

Throughout the Sermon on the Mount in Matthew 5-7 the Lord explains the divine standards of His kingdom. As the anointed Messiah, He has certain principles that He demands of those who want to enter His kingdom. Those principles are the thrust of the sermon, but they can all be summed up in one word: righteousness. Therefore, the whole sermon is summed up in Matthew 5:20: "I say unto you that except your righteousness shall exceed the righteousness of the scribes and Pharisees, ye shall in no case enter into the kingdom of heaven."

The kingdom of heaven is God's dominion. Entrance into that kingdom is dependent upon righteousness. How righteous do you need to be? Jesus says in Matthew 5:20 that you need to be more righteous than the scribes and Pharisees. How righteous were they? They were as righteous as man could get on his own terms. The scribes and Pharisees reached the epitome of human achievement in religion. They were obsessed with religious functions. The people around them believed they were exceedingly righteous. The scribes and Pharisees prayed, gave alms, and fasted. Their standards did not allow for murder or adultery. They maintained every minute element of the law. From man's perspective, they were righteous, but Christ demands a righteous-

74

ness that exceeds theirs. In fact, our Lord requires a righteousness that is beyond man's capacity to attain. It can only come from God.

2. The choices stated

That leaves people with two options: either they invent their own religion or they live God's way. They must decide whether to try to get to heaven on their own terms or to come on God's terms. The Sermon on the Mount climaxes at Matthew 7:13-14 when Jesus presents the two options: "Enter in at the narrow gate; for wide is the gate, and broad is the way, that leadeth to destruction, and many there be who go in that way; because narrow is the gate, and hard is the way, which leadeth unto life, and few there be that find it." Christ said that the broad gate leads to the broad way and destruction. It is the way of easy religion and human righteousness. The scribes, Pharisees, and other people who believe they are good enough to get to heaven travel that road. On the other hand, the narrow gate that precedes the narrow way leads to life. That is where the people with broken hearts and contrite spirits go. They know they can't keep God's standards and be perfect like Him. They cast themselves on the mercy of Christ, who gives them His own righteousness.

3. The complications specified

In the Lord's great invitation to enter the narrow gate, He showed that it is difficult to go through. Don't believe anyone who says that it is easy to become a Christian. It cost God everything—including His own Son— and it will cost you everything—including yourself. Those who offer cheap grace do people no favor; they delude them. It is difficult to come to God on His terms. You must recognize your inability to be righteous, which means getting rid of your pride. That's difficult to do, because people say that self is more important than anything else.

Let's look at why it is difficult to enter the narrow gate.

*a*) You must find it

The Lord says in Matthew 7:14, "Few there be that find it." The word *find* is important; it tells us that we have to search for the narrow gate. It requires effort. Jeremiah 29:13 says, "Ye shall seek me, and find me, when ye shall search for me with all your heart." No one stumbles into the kingdom of God inadvertently. You have to search for it.

*b*) You must leave the crowd

Many people are going the broad way. Few people go the narrow way. James said, "Whosoever, therefore, will be a friend of the world is the enemy of God" (4:4). John said, "If any man love the world, the love of the Father is not in him" (1 John 2:15). You have to leave the world's system to enter the narrow gate. That's difficult, because the crowd is going the other way. You have to enter alone. You can't come through with a group or a family.

*c*) You must enter unencumbered

To enter the narrow gate you must be stripped of self, sin, and self-righteousness. The narrow way is constricted. Christianity is a narrow life, and you must count the cost.

*d*) You must enter repentantly

You must agonize to enter the narrow gate. In the gospel of Luke Jesus says, "Strive to enter in at the narrow gate" (13:24). In other words, there must be penitence, confession, and a searching of one's soul.

*e*) You must beware of false prophets

In Matthew 7:15-20 Jesus says that false prophets add to the difficulty of entering the narrow gate. They stand at the crossroads trying to push people onto the broad road. They try to divert people for Satan's purposes. False prophets tell people that they can go to heaven with all their sin and selfishness and only pay a small price.

The Lord offered men an invitation. He said that the right decision is to enter the narrow gate, but it won't be easy. He said, "Few there be that find it" (Matt. 7:14).

## B. Exclusion from Heaven by Self-Deception

There is one other reason that only a few will walk the narrow way to life. Not only do false prophets deceive people, but people also deceive themselves. Self-deception keeps people from entering the narrow gate. J. C. Ryle, a nineteenth-century English pastor, wrote, "The Lord Jesus winds up the Sermon on the Mount by a passage of heart-piercing application. He turns from false prophets to false professors, from unsound teachers to unsound hearers" (*Expository Thoughts on the Gospels: St. Matthew* [Ipswich, Eng.: William Hunt, 1856], pp. 69-70). Bible commentator R. V. G. Tasker said, "It is not only false teachers who make the narrow way difficult to find and still harder to tread. A man may also be grievously self-deceived" (*The Gospel According to St. Matthew* [Grand Rapids: Eerdmans, 1977], p. 83). After Jesus presented the principles for entering the kingdom and warned about false prophets, it was fitting that He should end the sermon by saying, "Let me warn you about one more thing. Don't deceive yourself. Are you really a true member of the kingdom of heaven?"

### 1. The categories of self-deception

The Lord warned us about two categories of self-deception: mere verbal profession and mere intellectual knowledge. Matthew 7:21-23 discusses verbal profession: "Not everyone that saith" (v. 21), and, "Many will say to me" (v. 22). Jesus referred there to people who say they are Christians. Verses 24-27 discuss those who have only an intellectual knowledge: "Therefore, whosoever heareth these sayings" (v. 24), and, "Every one that heareth these sayings of mine" (v. 26). In verses 21-23 we see people who say they are Christians but don't do the Father's will, and in verses 24-27 we see people who hear God's commands but don't do them. All of those people are deceived. I call them people with empty

77

words and empty hearts. John Stott said that mere verbal profession and intellectual knowledge are "a camouflage for disobedience."

There is a key word at the end of verse 21: "Not every one . . . shall enter into the kingdom of heaven, but he that doeth the will of my Father, who is in heaven." Those who say they are Christians or hear what God says won't necessarily go to heaven. It is those who live a righteous life in Christ that will make it. The word *doeth* in verse 21 is a strong word.

The closing sections of the sermon (vv. 21-23, 24-27) contrast a right response with a wrong response to Christ's invitation. They show that our eternal destiny is determined by the choice we make. The next to the last section deals with what you say as opposed to what you do. The last section deals with what you hear as opposed to what you do. Keep in mind that the Lord was not speaking to irreligious people. He was speaking to people who were obsessed with religious activity. They weren't anti-God. The people Christ spoke to were religious, but they were damned because they were self-deluded and on the wrong road. Their delusion could have been caused by a false prophet, or they may have deluded themselves. Using Paul's words, they were people that had "a form of godliness, but [were] denying the power of it" (2 Tim. 3:5).

2. The caution about self-deception

   *a*) Emphasized

   I believe that we need to warn about self-delusion today, because the church of Jesus Christ is full of people who aren't Christians and don't know it. When I hear that two billion people in the world are Christians and two billion are not, I wonder what criteria are being used to determine who is a Christian. In a Gallup poll, 47 percent of the church-attending respondents said they had had a "born-again experience." About 25 percent of the unchurched respondents said the same (George Gallup, Jr., *The Search for America's Faith* [Nashville: Abingdon, 1980], p. 92).

Scripture says there will be few who believe. Some of the people who were polled may have deluded themselves into believing they were born again just because they said they were.

Jesus said many who believe they are Christians aren't. That is the ultimate delusion. You could be deluded about many things, but to be deceived into believing that you are a Christian when you aren't affects your eternal destiny. Christ said that you had better check yourself carefully. There are many deceived people in the church who believe everything is well. For them, judgment is going to be a big surprise. There is no better way to remove people's self-delusion than by teaching what Jesus says in the Sermon on the Mount. I believe that some of the deceived people in Matthew 7:21-27 are false prophets. Some of them know that they are phony, but others are probably self-deceived. However, those verses are also talking about many people who are self-deluded about whether or not they are redeemed.

The Bible is filled with warnings to people who are deceived. The reason there are so many warnings is because so many people are deceived: "Many will say to me in that day, Lord, Lord . . . ? And then will I profess unto them, I never knew you" (vv. 22-23). Not just a few people will be deceived.

*b)* Exemplified

Let's look at a warning that is similar to the one in Matthew 7. Matthew 25:1-12 says, "Then shall the kingdom of heaven be likened unto ten virgins, who took their lamps, and went forth to meet the bridegroom [the virgins are symbolic of people attached to Christianity, and the bridegroom represents Christ]. And five of them were wise, and five were foolish. They that were foolish took their lamps, and took no oil with them [i.e., they had a form of godliness but weren't really saved]; but the wise took oil in their vessels with their lamps. While the bridegroom tarried, they all slumbered and slept. And at midnight there was a cry made, Behold, the bridegroom com-

79

eth; go ye out to meet him. Then all those virgins arose and trimmed their lamps. And the foolish said unto the wise, Give us of your oil; for our lamps are gone out. But the wise answered, saying, Not so, lest there be not enough for us and you; but go rather to them that sell, and buy for yourselves. And while they went to buy, the bridegroom came, and they that were ready went in with him to the marriage; and the door was shut. Afterward came also the other virgins, saying, Lord, Lord, open to us. But he answered and said, Verily I say unto you, I know you not."

There is coming a day when people will expect the door to heaven to be open, but it will be shut forever. Jesus will say, "I don't know you." What a fearful thing! Many people who believe they are saved will be shocked at judgment time.

3. The causes of self-deception

What causes people to become deceived into believing they are saved? There are several ways that can happen.

*a*) A false doctrine of assurance

Sometimes people are told that if they say a special prayer and sign a card they will be saved. They are told not to question their salvation. That may give people false assurance. However, when you lead a person to Christ, you should never say, "I know you are saved; don't ever let anyone cause you to doubt that." Some people say, "If you ask Jesus into your life a second time, you are denying the permanence of the salvation God gave you. You are questioning God's integrity." That's not true. If you feel in your heart that you want to invite Jesus Christ to become the Lord and Savior of your life again, go ahead. Don't let someone else's false assurance take the place of conviction by the Spirit of God.

(1) The inadequacy of human assurance

Frequently people are told that because they said the right prayer and signed a card, they don't have to worry about whether or not they are saved. They are fooled into believing they are saved, when in reality the Spirit of God never was involved and their lives never changed. Don't tell a person, "I know you are saved because you did the right thing. Don't ever doubt your salvation." There is no way you can know if a person really came to know Christ. Don't risk giving someone mere psychological assurance.

(2) The importance of divine assurance

In the parable of the sower, when the seed of God's Word was cast on four kinds of soil, only one kind of soil manifested the fruit of true salvation (Matt. 13:1-8). Don't certify other people's salvation, or you might give them false assurance. Let God assure them through His Spirit. He witnesses with their spirits that they are the children of God (Rom. 8:16), whereby they'll cry, "Abba, Father" (Rom. 8:15). God will give them assurance when they "add to [their] faith virtue; and to virtue, knowledge; and to knowledge, self-control; and to self-control, patience; and to patience, godliness; and to godliness, brotherly kindness; and to brotherly kindness, love" (2 Pet. 1:5-7). When people manifest those things, then their election will be sure (2 Pet. 1:10)—they will know they have been forgiven of their sin. Let people have God's assurance of their salvation, not human certification. Many people believe they are saved because they were told that they are.

b) A failure to examine yourself

Some people are deceived because they never examine their lives. They think about God's grace and forgiveness so much that they never bother to face their sin. That can happen when people tell them, "You don't have to confess your sin; it's already been forgiven. Just keep living your life." That causes people to border on what is called antinomianism—an attitude of disregard for the law of God.

That's not right. Why do you believe the Lord asks us to celebrate Communion repeatedly (1 Cor. 11:26)? In order that we may examine our lives. Second Corinthians 13:5 says, "Examine yourselves, whether you are in the faith." If you don't do that, then you are in danger of self-deception. You need to look at your sin and examine your motives. If you are genuinely saved, God will confirm that by His Spirit witnessing with your spirit (Rom. 8:16). If that confirmation isn't there, don't believe you are saved simply because someone told you so.

c) A fixation on religious activity

Some people believe they are saved because they go to church, listen to sermons, sing songs, read their Bibles, and go to Bible studies. They are completely involved in religious activity. But that's a great illusion. There are many people like that in the church who are not saved. They are tares among the wheat (Matt. 13:24-30).

d) A fair-exchange approach

A form of self-delusion occurs when a person sees something wrong in his life and doesn't do anything about it but, rather, finds something right in his life and makes an exchange. Such a person will say, "I can't be that bad. Look at the good deed I recently did. That means I'm OK." That kind of person always trades off the bad and good deeds in his life. He never evaluates himself honestly to see if he is really a believer. He says, "I know I sinned, but I just did a good deed that will compensate for it." He whitewashes himself, never dealing with his sin.

You can deceive yourself by a false assurance, a failure to examine yourself, a fixation on religious activity, or a fair exchange approach.

It amazes me how many people are deceived. For example, I can't believe how many times I've encountered homosexuals who say to me, "We're Christians. We be-

82

lieve in Jesus." But the bottom line is this: Do you live in total obedience to the Word of God? Do you sense conviction when you disobey it and confess your sin to God? If you don't experience remorse over your sinfulness, it's fair to question whether you are a Christian.

## Deceived People: The Superficial and the Involved

There are two categories of deceived people in the church. These categories do not include hypocrites who know they are phony and try to appear religious. The first group of deceived people is the superficial, and the second group is the involved. The superficial people call themselves Christians because when they were young they went to church or Sunday school. Perhaps they got confirmed or "made a decision to accept Christ." Sometimes you hear people say at baptisms, "I received Christ when I was twelve years old, but my life was a mess after that. I want to go back to Christ." People who say that probably never received Christ when they were young. Some of them may believe they are Christians because they still go to church on Christmas and Easter and go to weddings and funerals.

The involved people are a much more subtle and serious group. They are involved in church and know the gospel, but they don't obey the Bible. Their lives are in a constant state of sinfulness.

4. The characteristics of self-deception

How can a person know if he is deceiving himself? How can we spot a self-deceived person? Let me give you a list of things to look for. Just because a person fits the description of one item on the list doesn't necessarily mean he is deceived. However, the things mentioned here are good indicators to go by.

*a*) Is the person seeking feelings, blessings, experiences, healings, and miracles? This person is probably more interested in the by-products of the faith than the faith itself. He seeks what he can get, not what he can glorify God for. He is more interested in pampering himself than in exalting Christ.

*b*) Is the person more committed to a denomination, church, or organization than he is to the Word of God? That person's Christianity may be purely social. He's the kind who says, "I've been a Lutheran all my life," or, "I'm a Presbyterian," or, "I belong to that church." He's more committed to the organization than to the Word of God.

*c*) Is the person involved in theology merely out of academic interest? You'll find this kind of person in colleges and seminaries. He studies theology and writes books about it. Theology for him is an intellectual activity. His life is devoid of the righteousness of Christ.

*d*) Does the person seem stuck on one particular point of theology? This is the person who bangs the proverbial drum for his favorite topic. Sometimes the area he emphasizes isn't even profound. He believes he is close to God and has great divine insight that no one else has. All of his activity is devoted to seeking attention to feed his ego. Watch out for a person that has a lack of balance in his theology.

*e*) Is the person overindulgent in the name of grace? A person who lacks penitence and a contrite heart is self-deceived.

All those people are self-deceived. They believe they are going to heaven, but they are on the broad road to destruction.

**Lesson**

In Matthew 7:21-27 the Lord warns those who are deceived. He speaks to those who believe they are on the right road but aren't. Verses 21-23 deal with the folly of empty words, and verses 24-27 deal with the folly of empty hearts.

I. THE FOLLY OF EMPTY WORDS (vv. 21-23)

Notice verses 21-22: "Not every one that saith unto me, Lord, Lord, shall enter into the kingdom of heaven, but he that doeth the will of my Father, who is in heaven. Many will say to me in that day, Lord, Lord, have we not prophesied in thy name? And in thy name have cast out demons? And in thy name done many wonderful works?" The claims are amazing and beautiful. But those people didn't do those things.

Elton Trueblood, a Protestant philosopher of religion, said, "Our main mission field today, as far as America is concerned, is within the church membership itself." Theologian Karl Barth, who wasn't evangelical but said some valuable things, remarked, "The true function of the church consists first of all in its own regeneration." The church is full of people who say empty words. They say they are Christians but don't do God's will. Romans 10:9 says, "If thou shalt confess with thy mouth the Lord Jesus, and shalt believe in thine heart that God hath raised him from the dead, thou shalt be saved." Confession is necessary, but confession without obedience is a sham.

A. The Conversation

1. The remarks of the self-deceived

a) "Lord, Lord"

The phrase "Lord, Lord" appears in verses 21-22. (The virgins in Matt. 25:1-12 used the same phrase in v. 11.) That's an interesting phrase. The first time it is said it's probably used as a term of respect or recognition. It means "Master," "Teacher," or "Sir." In a sense, the people are saying, "We respect You." The second time "Lord, Lord" is said may emphasize the orthodoxy of their claim. The word *Lord* (Gk., *kurios*) is used for the name *Jehovah* in the Septuagint (the Greek translation of the Old Testament). There the people are saying, "We know You are God. We accept all that Your deity involves: Your virgin birth, miraculous life, substitutionary death, powerful resurrection, intercession, and second coming." The people use the right terms and appear to have the right attitudes.

The fact that the people use the word *Lord* twice indicates their fervency. If the judgment spoken of here in Matthew 7 refers to the great white throne judgment, then those people will have already spent centuries in a place of punishment. That will add to their fervency. They will say, "Lord, why are we being punished?" They will address Christ with intensity and respect.

b) "In thy name"

In verse 22 the phrase "in thy name" is said three times. In other words, people will say to Jesus, "We preached for You. We cast out demons and did miracles for You. We did everything for You!" They will make amazing, orthodox claims. They will sound like Christians who were fervent in their private devotion and public ministry. There will be people who will truly be able to make that claim to Christ. The Lord will say, "You respected Me. You were fervent. You preached and worked for Me. Come into the kingdom" (Matt. 25:34-36). But not everyone who says that he did the will of the Father will enter heaven.

2. The response from the Lord

a) The confession

To those who did not do God's will, Jesus will say, "I never knew you; depart from me, ye that work iniquity" (v. 23). That was quoted from Psalm 6:8. Christ will say, "I want to confess to you that I never knew you." That's what was said to the virgins banging on the door in Matthew 25:11-12.

You may ask, "You mean God won't know who those people are?" No, God knows everything. We're not talking about an awareness of who someone is. In the Bible, the word *know* is often used to speak of an intimate relationship. For example, in Amos 3:2 God says to Israel, "You only have I known of all the families of the earth." He didn't mean that the Jewish people were the only people He knew; He was saying that He had an intimate relationship with them. In John 10 Jesus says, "My sheep hear my voice, and I know them." The best example would be in Genesis 4:17: "Cain knew his wife; and she conceived." The phrase "Cain knew his wife" doesn't mean he knew who she was or what her name was. It refers to his knowing her in the absolute, intimate act of marriage. When Mary became pregnant with the Lord by the Spirit of God, Joseph was shocked because he had never known her (Matt. 1:25). The word *know* embodies an intimate relationship. Jesus is saying in Matthew 7:23, "I never had an intimate relationship with you. Depart from Me."

*b)* The condemnation

Why does He ask them to depart from Him? According to the end of verse 23, they were those "that work iniquity." In other words, instead of doing the will of the Father, those people continually acted lawlessly. It isn't what you say that gets you into the kingdom; it's what you do. A profession of Christ is worthless if it isn't backed up by your life. In a sense, Peter said that if you can't add virtue to your faith, then you aren't truly redeemed (2 Pet. 1:5-10). James said, "Faith, if it hath not works, is dead" (2:17). Profession is valueless. In fact, I believe that to make an invalid profession of Christ is to take the Lord's name in vain. Using the Lord's name as street language is bad, but the epitome of violating God's name is to claim Christ when He isn't yours. Commentator G. Campbell Morgan said, "The blasphemy of the sanctuary is more awful than the blasphemy of the slum" (*The Gospel According to Matthew* [Old Tappan, N.J.: Revell, 1927], p. 79). To say, "Lord, Lord," and then disobey Him is like giving Him a Judas kiss.

*c)* The condition

We must be consumed with doing the will of God. That's why the disciples' prayer says, "Thy will be done in earth, as it is in heaven" (Matt. 6:10). We are responsible to let God's will be done through us. You may ask, "What if I fail?" The prayer goes on to say, "Forgive us our debts [trespasses], as we forgive our debtors" (v. 12). We know we are going to fail, and that's when we come to God for forgiveness. The righteous standard Jesus spoke of assumes that we will fail. But when we fail, we will confess it. First John 1:9 indicates that if we continually confess our sins, we give evidence that we are being forgiven. Only people who confess their sins are forgiven. When Jesus gave the Sermon on the Mount, He wasn't saying, "Here's the perfect standard. If you fail, you are out." He was saying, "Here's the perfect standard. When you fail, you deal with it." That's God's standard.

If the Sermon on the Mount is not the direction of your life, you are not a Christian. It doesn't matter if you say that you made some kind of confession or were baptized. In John 6:28 some people ask Jesus, "What shall we do, that we might work the works of God?" He answered, "This is the work of God, that ye believe on him whom he hath sent" (v. 29). Where do you start with the will of God? By believing in Christ. God wants all men to be saved (1 Tim. 2:3-4). The only thing acceptable to God is a righteousness that is the product of repentant faith in Jesus Christ. That produces good works. If that is not in your life, then you are not a Christian.

We can paraphrase the Lord's words in Matthew 7:23 to say, "I have never acknowledged you as My own or known you intimately. You are forever expelled from My presence because you continue to act lawlessly."

B. The Claims

Jesus' words are shocking because of the amazing claims made by the people He condemned. In verse 22 those people say, "Lord, Lord, have we not prophesied in thy name? And in thy name have cast out demons? And in thy name done many wonderful works?" There will be some people who will be able to make those claims legitimate. There have been true prophets. People have cast out demons in the name of Christ and have been empowered by God to do marvelous things. But there will be many who will make those claims untruthfully. Their claims will not get them into heaven.

Some people ask, "Did the people that will make those claims really preach, cast out demons, or do mighty works?" There are three possible alternatives: One, it's possible that they did—by God's power. Two, they may have done those things by Satan's power. Three, they may have faked what they did.

1. Enablement by God

Even if those people were unbelievers, could they have done those things? Yes. Did you know that God sometimes works through unbelievers? For example, Numbers 23:5 says, "The Lord put a word in Balaam's mouth." Peter said that "Balaam . . . loved the wages of unrighteousness" (2 Pet. 2:15). He was an evil prophet for hire, but God used his mouth. God worked through unregenerate people at the crucifixion of Christ. First Samuel 10:10 says of Saul, the apostate king of Israel, "The Spirit of God came upon him, and he prophesied." In John 11:51-52 the Lord puts a prophecy in the mouth of Caiaphas, a vile high priest. He prophesied that Christ would die for all men. It's possible that some of the self-deluded people in Matthew 7:22 were actually used by God.

2. Empowerment by Satan

It is also possible that self-deluded people did their preaching, exorcism, and wonderful works under the power of Satan. The devil can express his power. Do you remember what he did to Job? He brought death, destruction, and disease. God allowed the witch of Endor to conjure an evil spirit impersonating Samuel (1 Sam. 28:7-12). According to Acts 19:13-14, the sons of Sceva cast out demons. Jesus also acknowledged that some Jewish people had probably cast out demons when He said, "If I, by Beelzebub, cast out demons, by whom do your sons cast them out?" (Matt. 12:27). It's possible that some righteous Jewish people had cast out demons by the power of God, and some unrighteous Jewish people had done that through the power of Satan. You may ask, "Why would Satan cast out himself?" He is confused; his whole system is a mess. Deuteronomy 13 talks about false prophets who would prophesy signs and wonders that would happen. Those signs and wonders were probably energized by Satan. Matthew 24:24 says that false Christs and prophets will do signs and wonders, and 2 Thessalonians 2:8-10 says that the Antichrist will do them. Satan can do amazing things.

3. Employment of tricks

Some of what appears to be wonderful works is just fakery. In Exodus 7-8 the magicians of Egypt who tried to copy Moses' miracles are doing tricks.

The point is, the self-deluded people in Matthew 7:22 are going to say, "We preached, cast out demons, and did mighty works." Some of them may have been used by God to do what they did. They may have done their works by the devil's power, which masquerades as God's power. Or, they may have simply used fake magic, like most healers do today. It doesn't matter how they did it; what matters is that they were deceived. There are many people today who are preaching, casting out devils, and performing healings. They believe God is working through them. Other people who see them believe the same thing. However, their work is either energized by Satan or performed by trickery.

No matter what claims self-deceived people make, Jesus will say, "You are not qualified to be in My kingdom." Those people never came through the narrow gate. Making a mere verbal profession is not enough.

### Focusing on the Facts

1. What kind of righteousness does the Lord expect from those who want to enter heaven? Can people attain that righteousness? Explain (see pp. 75-76).
2. What two options does man have for trying to get to heaven (see p. 75)?
3. Explain why it is so difficult to enter the narrow gate (see pp. 76-77).
4. Not only do _____ _____ deceive people, but _____ also deceive _____ (see p. 77).

5. Name the two categories of self-deception. Explain what kind of people those categories speak of (see pp. 77-78).
6. What do the closing sections of the Sermon on the Mount speak of? Be specific (see p. 78).
7. What kind of people is the Lord speaking to in Matthew 7:21-27 (see p. 78)?
8. What is the ultimate delusion? What is the best way to remove a person's self-delusion (see pp. 78-79)?
9. What is wrong with telling someone that he is saved? How should a person receive assurance that he is saved (see pp. 80-81)?
10. Why does the Lord ask us to celebrate Communion repeatedly? What might happen to you if you don't do that (see p. 82)?
11. Explain the third thing that causes unsaved people to be under the delusion that they are saved (see p. 82).
12. What is the fair-exchange approach (see p. 82)?
13. What is the bottom line in determining whether you are a Christian (see p. 83)?
14. What reasons do superficial, deceived people give for calling themselves Christians? What are involved, deceived people like (see p. 83)?
15. What did Dr. Elton Trueblood say is our main mission field today? What is the first true function of the church, according to Karl Barth (see p. 85)?
16. What might the phrase "Lord, Lord" in Matthew 7-21-22 emphasize the first time it is said? What might it emphasize the second time? What does the fact that the word *Lord* is said twice indicate (see pp. 85-86)?
17. In Matthew 7:23 Jesus says, "I never knew you." Does that mean He was never aware of them? Explain (see pp. 86-87).
18. Why will Jesus ask the people in Matthew 7:21-23 to depart from Him (see p. 87)?
19. What makes a profession of Christ worthless? What do you do when you make an invalid profession of Christ (see p. 87)?
20. What are we to be consumed with? What are we to do if we fail in doing that? What do we give evidence of if we respond properly when we fail (see pp. 87-88)?
21. What is the only kind of righteousness that is acceptable to God (see p. 88)?
22. The people in Matthew 7:22 make some amazing claims. Specify those claims. What three possible alternatives explain how those self-deceived people did what they did (see pp. 88-90)?
23. Give some examples of how God has worked through unbelievers. Support your answers with Scripture (see pp. 89-90).

24. Can Satan help people do miraculous things? Explain, using Scripture to support your answer (see p. 89).
25. Why will Jesus tell the self-deceived people in Matthew 7:22, "You are not qualified to be in My kingdom" (see p. 90)?

## Pondering the Principles

1. Read Philippians 3:4-9. In verse 4 Paul says that if a person could get to heaven by his own righteousness, he is well qualified. Before Paul became saved, what did he believe gave him the right to go to heaven (vv. 5-6)? How did Paul feel about those things after he became saved (vv. 8-9)? What was Paul's desire, according to verse 9? What attitude do you have about your works of righteousness? Are you guilty of using the fair-exchange approach mentioned on page 82? Do you believe your righteous deeds earn you God's blessing? Examine yourself, and make sure that you have the right perspective on the righteous works in your life. True righteousness is a product of repentant faith in Jesus Christ. Give God the credit for what He produces in your life.

2. Read James 2:14-17. What point do verses 14 and 17 make? Read the example James gives in verses 15-16 to support his statement in verse 14. Have you ever noticed a Christian brother or sister in need and not provided help? Why? Do the things you do truly manifest a saving faith in Christ? If you are a Christian, ask God to give you opportunities to back up your professed faith in Christ with good works.

3. Read the list of characteristics found in self-deceived people on pages 83-84. Remember that just because one trait is present in a person it doesn't necessarily mean that he is self-deceived. However, it could be an indication of self-deception. Taking each item on the list, answer the following question: If you met a person with that trait, what would you say to help correct him? Going over that list again, do you find any of those traits in you? Make sure that in your Christian walk you don't stress feelings and miracles, advocate denominationalism, let yourself be obsessed with academics or a favorite theological topic, or indulge in God's grace without penitence.

# 5
# Empty Words and Empty Hearts—Part 2

## Outline

Introduction
A. The Scene
   1. Catastrophes in California
   2. Catastrophes in Palestine
B. The Story

Review
I. The Folly of Empty Words (vv. 21-23)

Lesson
II. The Folly of Empty Hearts (vv. 24-27)
   A. The Discussion
      1. The two builders
         a) The similarities detailed
         b) The difference detected
      2. The true believer
         a) His foundation
            (1) Identified
            (2) Illustrated
         b) His function
            (1) Delineated in Scripture
            (2) Delineated in the Sermon
   B. The Distinctions
      1. The foolish man
         a) He is in a hurry
         b) He is superficial
      2. The wise man
         a) He is not in a hurry
         b) He gives maximum effort
         c) He is teachable

C.  The Destruction
  1.  The inevitability of condemnation
      *a*)  Described in Matthew
      *b*)  Described in Revelation
  2.  The importance of consecration
      *a*)  1 Corinthians 6:9-10
      *b*)  Galatians 5:19-21
      *c*)  Revelation 21:8

Conclusion
A.  The People's Response to the Sermon
B.  Your Response to the Sermon

## Introduction

A.  The Scene

  1.  Catastrophes in California

      In Southern California, people are constantly made aware of the need for good foundations in their homes. They may frequently encounter earthquakes or floods. Earthquakes crack foundations, and floods wash them away. Living in Southern California can be interesting, especially in earthquake- or flood-prone areas. Whenever a house is built, the builder has to keep in mind the possibility that an earthquake or a flood could occur at any time. Careful soil tests are done, and the soil is compacted to make sure that the foundation is going to stand.

  2.  Catastrophes in Palestine

      The climate in Palestine is almost identical to that of Southern California. Most of the time it is dry. But when it rains, the ground can't absorb all the water, and a flood often results. Houses are easily washed away, just as they are in Southern California. When designing a building, the people have to prepare the ground so that the foundation will be strong. What looks like a wonderful place to build in the summer may become a raging river in the winter, wiping away whatever has been

94

placed there. That's what Jesus had in mind in Matthew 7:24-27.

B. The Story

In the closing paragraph of His sermon, Christ pictures two men, each building a home. Perhaps they were building on a dry streambed in a valley. One man works feverishly to build his house and does not think about a solid foundation to withstand future flooding. He is the "foolish man" (v. 26). The other man builds his house on a foundation of solid rock. He is the "wise man" (v. 24). Jesus' story is simple: there are two men building houses. One is wise, and one is foolish. What appears to be a simple story, however, is really a shocking, powerful commentary on people who know Jesus' words but have an empty heart. Notice verse 24, where Jesus says, "Whosoever heareth," and verse 26, where He says, "Every one that heareth." Christ was talking about people who hear His message and understand it. Wise people do something about it, but fools don't. James Denney said, "It is the consciousness that the speaker is nothing less than the final judge of all which makes the parable of the builders on rock and sand the most solemn and overpowering."

In Matthew 7:13-14 Jesus begins closing His Sermon on the Mount with an invitation. He tells us, in effect, to enter through the narrow gate onto the narrow way that leads to life. He says that won't be easy for two basic reasons: false prophets will deceive many, and many people will falsely profess Christ and deceive themselves. We all live under some illusions; we cultivate most of them ourselves. It's a tendency of human nature to try to cover up faults.

The Lord says that you must enter the narrow gate, and that it won't be easy because false prophets try to send people onto the broad way (vv. 15-20). It also won't be easy because people tend to deceive themselves. In verses 21-23 Christ says there will be people who verbally profess to belong in the kingdom, but won't do what Christ said. The dichotomy indicates that they are not true Christians. Then in verses 24-27, the Lord talks about those who know His message but have empty hearts. The first group has empty words, and the second group has empty hearts. People will deceive themselves either way: they will profess that they are Christians and convince themselves of that even though there is no evidence in their lives. Or they will have mere knowledge that seems to suffice for a real heart relationship. Some people are deceived into believing they are Christians because they know so much about Christianity. Others believe they are Christians because they talk so much about Christianity.

## Review

I. THE FOLLY OF EMPTY WORDS (vv. 21-23; see pp. 84-90)

## Lesson

II. THE FOLLY OF EMPTY HEARTS (vv. 24-27)

In Matthew 7:24-27 the Lord reminds us that we must meet God's standard of righteousness if we are to enter the kingdom of God. Unless your life is built on His standard, you'll be washed away by the flood. It doesn't matter how much you know or how feverishly you conduct your spiritual activity.

A. The Discussion

1. The two builders

Notice verse 24, which begins, "Whosoever heareth these sayings of mine," and verse 26, which begins, "Every one that heareth these sayings of mine." The Lord was referring to people who have heard His message. Then at the end of verses 24 and 26, we read of two men building their houses. They have listened to the message and are involved in spiritual activity. They both belong to the visible body of believers. Both men probably read Scripture, attend meetings at a church, and go by a spiritual value system. However, there is one tremendous difference: one man is wise because he builds on rock, and the other man is foolish because he builds on sand. By the way, once the edifice is up, you can't see the foundation anymore. Thus, it becomes difficult to tell what kind of foundation exists under the building. True Christians can be deceived about who truly is and is not a Christian. What the Lord is saying is simple. Many people hear Christ's teaching; but it's those who obey His teaching that get into the kingdom. That's the bottom line. If you examine your life and find that you are a hearer and not a doer, don't deceive yourself into believing you are a Christian (James 1:22-25). Jesus said the storm that comes along will manifest the truth about who is wise and who is foolish.

*a*) The similarities detailed

There are several similarities in the story of the two builders. First, both men build a house. They are both involved in spiritual activity that has to do with the kingdom of God. Second, both individuals build their houses in the same location. We know that because both houses are subject to the same storm. True believers and false believers invariably live side by side. They attend the same church and Bible study. Third, both of their buildings are so similar that they are indistinguishable to most people. In fact, both men build their homes the same way, because the Lord said the only difference is in their foundations. Both men build houses in the same location, and they build them in the same way. Both individuals carry a Bible and notebook; both of them pray, give, and participate in certain activities. All they do appears identical. The only difference is their foundations. Unfortunately, those are not visible once the edifice is up. Only an honest, soul-searching examination can reveal the truth. That's what Jesus tried to get the Pharisees to do. He wanted them to get off their high tower, look at their lives, and see how spiritually bankrupt they were.

*b*) The difference detected

Verse 24 says that one man "built his house upon a rock [Gk., *petra*, "a rock bed"]." There is another Greek word, *petros*, that means "a stone or a boulder." The wise man built his house on a rock bed. Verse 26 says the other man "built his house upon the sand [Gk., *ammon*]." That is, he built his house on sand like that found on a seashore.

A man is wise if he builds on a rock bed, and a man is foolish if he builds on shifting sands of the sea or desert. The false prophets mentioned in verses 15-20 are real estate agents trying to sell sand lots! It is foolish to build on sand, because when a storm comes it will wash away the sand under the house. Verse 27 says that a house built on sand will fall. But a house built on a solid foundation of rock will not fall in a storm.

---

**Spirituality on Shifting Sands**

In the story about the two builders, Jesus rebukes the religion of the Pharisees. They had no regard for spirituality of soul, purity of heart, integrity of behavior, or obedience to God. They were building their spiritual structure on sand. It's true that the Pharisees prayed, fasted, and gave alms, but they only did those things to parade their supposed spirituality and enhance their reputations. Their religion of externals was based on sand. They didn't go through the narrow gate. The broad way that leads to destruction is all sand.

---

2. The true believer

   *a*) His foundation

   (1) Identified

   A wise person builds his life on rock (v. 24). What does it mean to build your life on rock? We could say that the rock is God and that you are literally building your life on God. Psalm 18:2 says, "The Lord is my rock." The Pharisees claimed that their lives were built on God. We could also say the rock is Christ. Peter mentioned that Christ is the chief cornerstone (1 Pet. 2:6). Paul said Christ is the rock (1 Cor. 10:4). There is more to building on the rock, however, than just saying your life is built on Christ. Most commentators say that the rock is God or Christ. But a careful look at Matthew 7:24 and 26 shows us what the rock is. Jesus said, "Whosoever heareth these sayings of mine, and doeth them, I will liken him unto a wise man, who built his house upon a rock" (v. 24). It is the people who hear *and* do what Christ commanded that build their house on the rock. It's true that God is a rock and Christ is the chief cornerstone, but the Lord was saying that His words are the foundation of the true church.

(2) Illustrated

Matthew 16 is a familiar text that aptly illustrates what I am saying. Verses 13-18 say, "When Jesus came into the borders of Caesarea Philippi [the extreme northern part of Israel], he asked his disciples, saying, Who do men say that I, the Son of man, am? And they said, Some say that thou art John the Baptist; some, Elijah; and others, Jeremiah, or one of the prophets. He saith unto them, But who say ye that I am? And Simon Peter answered and said, Thou art the Christ, the Son of the living God. And Jesus answered and said unto him, Blessed art thou, Simon Barjona; for flesh and blood hath not revealed it unto thee, but my Father, who is in heaven [i.e., Peter had received a divine revelation]. And I say also unto thee, That thou art Peter [Gk., *petros*, "pebble" or "boulder"], and upon this rock [Gk., *petra*, "rock bed foundation"] I will build my church" (vv. 13-18). Peter said to Christ, "Thou art the Christ, the Son of the living God" (v. 16). Christ in effect responded, "Upon that affirmation of truth I will build my church." The word *petra* in Matthew 16:18 refers to the Word of God. It means the same thing in Matthew 7:24. In Acts 20:32 Paul says, "I commend you . . . to the word of his grace, which is able to build you up." The Word of God is our foundation, and it provides us with the materials we need for building.

The Lord was saying that the person who only hears God's Word but doesn't act on it is building on sand. The sand represents human will, opinion, and attitudes. A foolish person builds his life on the shifting sands of human philosophy. He only listens to Christ's words; therefore, he is not established on the rock. But the wise man who hears God's Word and builds his life on it is building on a rock foundation. He lives a life of obedience. John 8:30 says that as Jesus spoke "many believed on him." They listened to Christ. In verse 31 Jesus says, "If ye continue in my word, then are ye my disciples indeed." If we only hear and believe, that doesn't mean anything. It's when we continue to obey the Word of God that we build our lives on the rock. Don't be deceived because of your verbal claims. Unless you build your life on biblical truth you are deceiving yourself.

*b)* His function

(1) Delineated in Scripture

James 1:22 says, "Be ye doers of the word and not hearers only, deceiving your own selves." The Lord was saying the same thing in the Sermon on the Mount. Verses 23-24 continue, "For if any be a hearer of the word, and not a doer, he is like a man beholding his natural face in a mirror; for he beholdeth himself, and goeth his way, and immediately forgetteth what manner of man he was." In other words, if you are not a doer of the Word, then it is not having any effect on your life or destiny. Colossians 1:21, 23 says, "You, that were once alienated and enemies in your mind by wicked works, yet now hath he reconciled . . . if ye continue in the faith grounded and settled." First John 2:3 says, "By this we do know that we know him, if we keep his commandments." Both the Lord and the apostles stated the importance of obeying God's Word. Titus 1:16 says, "They [unbelievers] profess that they know God, but in works they deny him, being abominable, and disobedient." If you verbally profess to be a Christian and know some things about Christianity but there is no obedience in your life, then you are not saved.

Building your life on the rock means being obedient. Examine your life. Do you desire, more than anything else, to obey the Word of God? Or do you live in disobedience and try to justify yourself? Obedience is the key word here. The only validation you will ever have of your salvation is a life of obedience. That is the only way you can prove that you really recognize the lordship of Jesus Christ. If you do not obey God's Word, your confession of Christ as Lord is a mere verbal exercise.

(2) Delineated in the Sermon

The life that is built on the rock is the kind of life that is described in the Sermon on the Mount. A true believer has a biblical view toward self and lives out the Beatitudes (Matt. 5:3-12). A person who builds his life on the rock preserves the world and lights it up without being a part of it (5:13-16). He doesn't seek to alter the Bible but accepts it (5:17-20). Such a person has biblical moral standards (5:21-32). He doesn't try to get away with everything he can. His Christianity is internal, not external. He has a biblical attitude toward words (5:33-37), deeds (5:38-47), motives (6:1-18), money (6:19-24), things (6:25-34), and people (7:1-12). Jesus spoke about all of those things in His sermon. He says in Matthew 7:24 that if you are committed to obedience you are building on the rock.

## The Marks of True Salvation

When I hear someone say, "I am a born-again believer, but I live the way I always have," I question whether he is really a Christian. I recently read an article in a magazine that discussed what pastors should do with unmarried Christians who live together. If two such people are living together, I doubt that they are Christians. We don't need to re-evaluate the standards for marriage; we need to establish the standard for who is really a Christian. If you are not obedient to the principles in the Sermon on the Mount, you are probably self-deceived. You don't become a Christian just by making a decision, raising your hand, or signing a card. True salvation is marked by a recognition of God's divine standards, experiencing an overwhelming sense of sinfulness, and pleading for God to be merciful and give you His righteousness because you desire to live for Him. You can't say, "I want to come to Christ and be saved, but I don't want to worry about being obedient." If you say that, you are not a Christian. It grieves me to hear a Christian say, "I know so-and-so is saved, but he never comes to church and is not interested in it." If that is true, the person is probably self-deceived.

Let's examine the self-delusion that is presented in Matthew 7:24-27 more carefully. We've already seen the similarities between the wise man and the fool.

B. The Distinctions

1. The foolish man

One man built his house the easy way, and the other one built his the hard way. It's easy to build on sand because you don't have to dig. That's the way life is on the broad road: you can do anything you want; you can carry all your garbage with you. A fool builds the easy way for two reasons.

*a*) He is in a hurry

Fools are always in a hurry. The book of Proverbs says that a fool "maketh haste" (28:20). Over the years I have learned that I am not good at building things. At the same time, I've learned that if you do something right the first time, you won't have to do it again.

It's easy to build on sand because you don't have to dig. A fool always looks for shortcuts and quick results. He does not take time for building a sense of conviction, cultivating a deep awareness of God, and listening to the doctrine of sin. A foolish person does not come to grips with his sinfulness before God. The world today has a quick, canned approach to everything. Some people are in such a hurry that if they don't get their hamburger at a fast food place in three minutes, they get very upset! Quick evangelism attracts more fools than wise men. However, no one should build a tower until he has counted the cost (Luke 14:28).

*b*) He is superficial

There are many people who say they believe in Christ and accept the gospel yet give no evidence in their lives to confirm that. They are superficial. We live in the age of superficiality: millions of people profess to be Christians, but when they don't get what they want from Christ and their houses begin to collapse, they look for another sandy place to build.

I become irritated when I hear a superficial presentation of Christ that is supposed to be legitimate. Some preach sermons that have nothing to do with the gospel and afterward invite people to come forward to accept their message. But it includes no foundation and no brokenness of heart. Arthur Pink said, "If I have never mourned over my waywardness, I have no solid ground for rejoicing" (*An Exposition of the Sermon on the Mount* [Grand Rapids: Baker, 1952]). Charles Spurgeon said, "Want of depth, want of sincerity, want of reality in religion—this is the want of our times. Want of an eye to God in religion, lack of sincere dealing with one's soul, neglect of using the lancet with our hearts, neglect of the search warrant which God gives out against sin, carelessness concerning living upon Christ; much reading about Him, much talking about Him, but too little feeding upon His flesh, and drinking of His blood—these are the causes of tottering professions and baseless hopes" (*Spurgeon's Expository Encyclopedia*, vol. 4 [Grand Rapids: Baker, 1977], p. 226).

2. The wise man

Although the foolish man is in a hurry, the wise man is not. In Luke 6:46-49, which is a parallel passage, we read that the wise man "dug deep" (v. 48). He dug for the rock—God's Word—and blew away the sand of human opinion and self-will.

*a*) He is not in a hurry

A wise man is not a quick convert who makes a superficial confession of sin. Arthur Pink said, "There are some who say they are saved before they have any sense they are lost" (*An Exposition of the Sermon on the Mount* [Grand Rapids: Baker, 1953]). Some people present the gospel so poorly that even unbelievers don't know enough to reject it! Those who claim Christ as their own are willing to dig deep. They have thought out the responsibility involved. They don't rush into confessing Christ as Lord only to depart later on. A wise person counts the cost (Luke 14:28). He considers what he is doing. He digs deep and is not in a hurry.

When the Lord sows the seed in the parable in Matthew 13, he says, "He that received the seed in stony places, the same is he that heareth the word, and immediately with joy receiveth it; yet hath he not root in himself, but endureth for a while; for when tribulation or persecution ariseth because of the word, immediately he is offended" (vv. 20-21). I've seen that happen many times. A person will say, "I'm a Christian," but as soon as the demands of God's Word are made clear to him, he is gone. That's not the way it is with the person who digs deep to the rock bed of God's Word so that he might obey. He isn't superficial.

*b*) He gives maximum effort

Those who dig deep show a desire to give maximum effort. People are always drawn to the easy path. Some people make the requirements of the gospel so easy that their converts are not really saved. They say, "It is so difficult to follow up converts!" In one year, one large church in America had 28,000 people who professed their conversion on paper and 9,600 people who were baptized. Yet only 123 people were added to the church. One man on the staff of that church said, "I knew something had to be wrong. So I left and asked God to show me what was right." There were not 28,000 conversions if only 123 people were added to the church. The problem is not the difficulty of follow up; it's the difficulty of true conversion. We can't follow up people who were never redeemed. People sometimes say, "We must get converts into a follow-up program. We can't just leave them to the Holy Spirit!" However, if a person is truly converted, God will do His work. It's impossible to follow up an unconverted person.

The person who digs deep strives to enter through the narrow gate (Luke 13:24). He minimizes his travail of soul because he wants to build on the rock. It's much easier to go the way of the flesh. It's hard to restrict yourself and go God's way. But His commandments are not grievous; they are blessed (1 John 5:3). We obey them out of love, not out of duty to law.

*c*) He is teachable

The man who digs deep wants to do things right. He is teachable. The Pharisees weren't teachable; you couldn't tell them anything. There are many people like that. They profess Christ, but they don't want to count the cost of following Him and being obedient. That kind of people want to live with their own ideas, goals, and will. When you try to teach them what is right they don't listen. It's not because they are unteachable Christians; it's because they aren't Christians at all.

The person who digs deep gets rid of his self-righteousness and self-sufficiency. He knows he is not commendable and is overwhelmed with his sin. He strives to enter through the narrow gate—he places Scripture in his heart so that he won't sin against God (Ps. 119:11). Such a person is interested in a genuine love relationship with God, not a routine of spiritual activity. He does not build on visions, experiences, or miracles but on God's Word. He builds for God's glory, not his own.

## C. The Destruction

### 1. The inevitability of condemnation

Many people want spiritual power. In Acts 8:18-21 a man named Simon wants to buy the power of the Holy Spirit. Peter told him, "Thy money perish with thee . . . for thy heart is not right in the sight of God" (vv. 20-21). There are people who want spiritual power, but they aren't interested in living according to God's standards. They are building on sand. They want the good things Jesus can give them without being committed to Him. Eventually, according to Matthew 7:25 and 27, the day of reckoning will come.

#### *a*) Described in Matthew

Matthew 7:25 and 27 basically talk about the whole of judgment. I don't believe a person can say, "The rain represents this, the flood refers to that, the wind means that, and the beating on the house represents that." A person can get carried away trying to analyze those things. Jesus is simply saying that one day a storm came, and the house on the sand fell, while the house on the rock stood. Someday there is going to be a divine accounting. God will send the wind, rain, and flood of judgment. Some will stand through the storm while others will fall. Whether your religion is true or false, you will encounter that storm. Whether you are chaff or wheat will be found out. Someday the chief Winnower will come, and He will separate the chaff from the wheat (Matt. 3:12). He will blow the wind of judgment, and those who built their lives on the rock will stand (Matt. 7:25). Paul told the Thessalonians that Jesus has "delivered us from the wrath to come" (1 Thess. 1:10). Why did he say that? Because their faith was genuine (1:4).

#### *b*) Described in Revelation

There is going to come a judgment time. Revelation 20 gives these details: "I saw a great white throne, and him that sat on it, from whose face the earth and the heaven fled away, and there was found no place for them. And I saw the dead, small and great, stand before God, and the books were opened; and another book was opened, which is the book of life. And the dead were judged out of those things which were written in the books, according to their works. And the sea gave up the dead that were in it, and death and hades delivered up the dead that were in them; and they were judged every man according to their works. And death and hades were cast into the lake of fire. This is the second death. And whosoever was not found written in the book of life was cast into the lake of fire" (vv. 11-15). That is the second death. Whoever's name is not found in the book of life will be thrown into the lake of fire. That passage describes the great white throne judgment, when God separates false believers from the true for eternity. Echoing the halls of judgment will be the cries of the self-deceived, "Lord, Lord," and the reverberation of the Lord's reply, "Depart from me, I never knew you."

People are deluded. Satan is a liar. He is a deceiver, and his ultimate deception is to lead someone to believe he is a Christian when he is not. If you don't know that you have a problem, you won't be looking for the answer to that problem. The day of judgment is coming. You had better examine your life. Matthew 7:21 says that not everyone who believes he is going to heaven will end up there. Examine your foundation. You may respect Christ and be orthodox. You may be active in private devotion and public proclamation. You may be building a religious life in the same community that true believers dwell. Your house may look exactly like theirs. But when judgment comes it will fall down because it is built on the sand of your own will. I tell you this from my heart: go back and check your foundation.

Jesus' unequaled, masterful Sermon on the Mount ends with a devastating warning about judgment. The final words in the sermon are, "And great was the fall of [the house]" (7:27). Every time you present the gospel you must end your presentation with a warning of doom to the person who rejects it. Don't just say, "If you don't come to Christ, you are missing many nice things." You must call for a decision.

2. The importance of consecration

You may say, "I chose Christ. I chose the right way." Proverbs 30:12 says, "There is a generation that are pure in their own eyes, and yet are not washed from their filthiness." Some people believe they are washed from their sin. You may ask, "How can I know if I am washed?" See what your life is built on. Check to see if you are in any of the lists below.

a) 1 Corinthians 6:9-10—"Know ye not that the unrighteous shall not inherit the kingdom of God? Be not deceived: neither fornicators, nor idolaters, nor adulterers, nor effeminate, nor abusers of themselves with mankind, nor thieves, nor covetous, nor drunkards, nor revilers, nor extortioners, shall inherit the kingdom of God." Look at your life.

b) Galatians 5:19-21—"The works of the flesh are manifest, which are these: adultery, fornication, uncleanness, lasciviousness, idolatry, sorcery, hatred, strife, jealousy, wrath, factions, seditions, heresies, envyings, murders, drunkenness, revelings, and the like; of which I tell you before, as I have also told you in time past, that they who do such things shall not inherit the kingdom of God." Don't be deceived.

c) Revelation 21:8—"But the fearful, and unbelieving, and the abominable, and murderers, and fornicators, and sorcerers, and idolaters, and all liars, shall have their part in the lake which burneth with fire and brimstone, which is the second death."

Do you see yourself in any of those lists? I know that we all sin, but that's not what I'm talking about. If any of those things are characteristic of your life, you are not living in the kingdom. It doesn't matter what you believe; that's what the Word of God says. Remember, Matthew 7:14 says, "Few there be that find [the narrow gate]." When you do give your life to the Lord, however, He takes over, empowers you, and changes you. Paul said, "He who hath begun a good work in you will perform it until the day of Jesus Christ" (Phil. 1:6).

## Conclusion

### A. The People's Response to the Sermon

What was the response to Jesus' sermon? Was there a great revival with many converts? No. Matthew 7:28-29 says, "It came to pass, when Jesus had ended these sayings, the people were astonished at his doctrine; for he taught them as one having authority, and not as the scribes." All the listeners did was analyze the sermon. They "were astonished" (v. 28). The Greek word for that literally means "they were struck out of their senses." They were amazed that someone could say those things with such power and authority. Jesus didn't do what the scribes did; they merely quoted other people. They were fallible, and they quoted other fallible people to back up what they said. Jesus said things on the basis of His own authority. No one had ever seen such wisdom. Every dimension of human life was discussed in an economy of words that was breathtaking. No one had ever heard such deep insight about the law of God or the sin of man. The listeners around Jesus had never heard anyone confront the Jewish religious leaders the way Jesus did. They were shocked that Jesus stood on His own authority and not someone else's.

The people who heard Jesus' sermon had never heard anyone speak the truth as He did. Divine matters were spoken of with great clarity. They had never heard anyone speak with such love. But they didn't respond the right way. Those people couldn't believe that a man would call Himself the fulfillment of the law and the determiner of righteousness. They couldn't believe that the scribes and Pharisees needed correcting. Those who heard Jesus had a hard time accepting His claim that He was God, the way of life, and the Judge of all. They couldn't believe that He was the King. Their response was one of astonishment.

B. Your Response to the Sermon

You don't need to have the same reaction that those people did to the Sermon on the Mount. You should be more than shocked; you should desire to be converted. That's what Jesus is after. What is your response to His words? Your eternal destiny depends on it!

Edward Mote wrote this in the hymn "The Solid Rock":

> In every high and stormy gale
> My anchor holds within the veil.
> When all around my soul gives way,
> He then is all my hope and stay.
> On Christ the solid Rock, I stand;
> All other ground is sinking sand.

Your life is built on either rock or sand. You are either obedient or disobedient. That is the only way to verify whether your faith is legitimate. I pray that your faith is built on Christ.

### Focusing on the Facts

1. What is the simple story in Matthew 7:24-27 really a commentary on (see p. 95)?
2. What similarities are there between the two builders in Matthew 7:24-27 (see pp. 95-96)?
3. What is the only difference between the two builders? Why is it difficult to spot that difference (see pp. 96-97)?
4. What does the Greek word *petra* in Matthew 7:24 mean? What kind of sand is referred to in verse 26 (see pp. 97-98)?
5. Whom does Jesus rebuke through the story of the two builders? Why (see p. 98)?
6. What exactly is the rock a person should build his life on (Matt. 7:24; see pp. 98-99)?
7. What does the sand in Matthew 7:26 represent (see pp. 99-100)?
8. What distinction could be made between the people in John 8:30 and the people in John 8:31 (see p. 100)?
9. According to James 1:22, what do you do to yourself if you are only a hearer of the Word? According to James 1:23-24, what happens to a man who is not a doer of the Word (see p. 100)?

10. What is the only validation you will ever have of your salvation (see p. 101)?
11. What marks true salvation (see pp. 101-2)?
12. What is the first reason that a fool builds the easy way? How does that affect his perspective on sin and God (see pp. 102-3)?
13. What is wrong with superficial presentations of the gospel (see p. 103)?
14. Give three characteristics of a wise man (see pp. 103-5).
15. What is a wise person's approach to acknowledging Christ as Lord (Luke 14:28; see p. 104)?
16. What does the person who digs deep empty himself of? What is he interested in? What does he not build on (see p. 105)?
17. What does the storm in Matthew 7:25, 27 represent (see p. 106)?
18. What wonderful promise is made to believers in 1 Thessalonians 1:10 (see p. 106)?
19. Every time you present the gospel, how should you end your presentation (see pp. 107-8)?
20. What point is being made in Proverbs 30:12 (see p. 108)?
21. Why did the people who heard Christ's sermon respond with astonishment (Matt. 7:28-29; see p. 109)?
22. What kind of response should people have to Christ's sermon (see p. 110)?

### Pondering the Principles

1. If you have truly responded to Christ's invitation to enter the narrow gate, that will be manifest by the way you live. Christ implicitly says in Matthew 7:24-27 that those who hear Him but don't obey will be condemned. Read the following verses one at a time, and discuss what they teach about obedience: Leviticus 20:8; Deuteronomy 13:4; Ecclesiastes 12:13; Matthew 19:17; John 13:17; 14:15, 21; and Ephesians 6:6-7. Are you wholeheartedly obedient to God's Word? Why is it important for us to be obedient?

2. Read 1 Thessalonians 1:1-10. Find all the reasons that Paul was thankful for the believers at Thessalonica. If Paul had to write a commentary about your obedience to God, what do you believe he would say? Are there things in your life that need to be changed? Clarify in your mind what you need work on in your

life, and commit yourself to cultivating an obedient life that will please God.

3. How would you describe your relationship with God? Is it deep and intimate or is it superficial? Are your prayers always short and repetitive? Do you involve yourself in church activities without cultivating a personal relationship with God? What kind of fruit (actions) does your life manifest? In 2 Corinthians 13:5 Paul says, "Examine yourselves, whether you are in the faith; prove yourselves." Spend time with God in earnest prayer and examine your spiritual foundation before Him.

# Scripture Index

# Topical Index